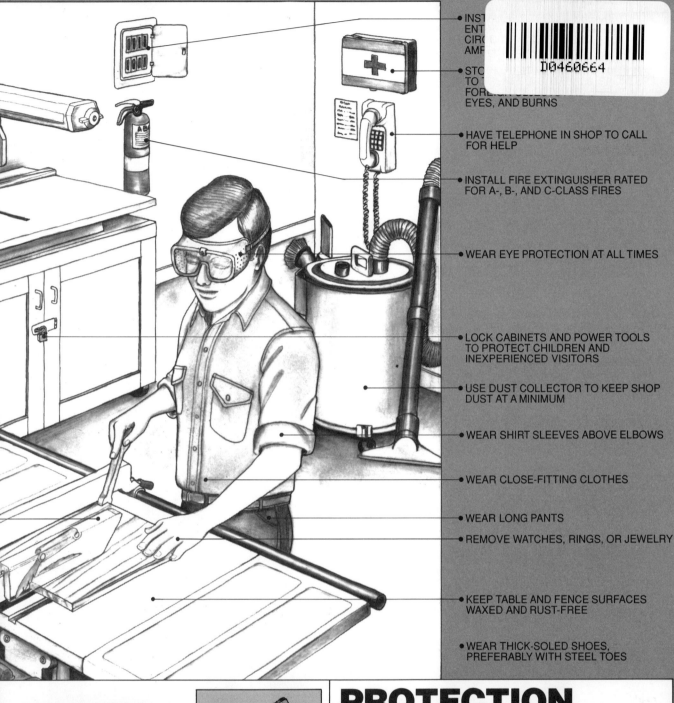

- INST... ENT... CIRC... AMP...

- STO... TO T... FOREIGN... EYES, AND BURNS

- HAVE TELEPHONE IN SHOP TO CALL FOR HELP

- INSTALL FIRE EXTINGUISHER RATED FOR A-, B-, AND C-CLASS FIRES

- WEAR EYE PROTECTION AT ALL TIMES

- LOCK CABINETS AND POWER TOOLS TO PROTECT CHILDREN AND INEXPERIENCED VISITORS

- USE DUST COLLECTOR TO KEEP SHOP DUST AT A MINIMUM

- WEAR SHIRT SLEEVES ABOVE ELBOWS

- WEAR CLOSE-FITTING CLOTHES

- WEAR LONG PANTS

- REMOVE WATCHES, RINGS, OR JEWELRY

- KEEP TABLE AND FENCE SURFACES WAXED AND RUST-FREE

- WEAR THICK-SOLED SHOES, PREFERABLY WITH STEEL TOES

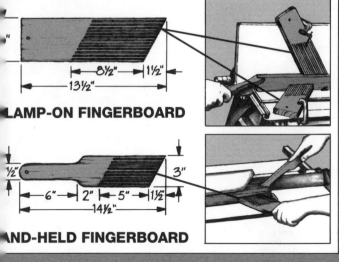

8½" | 1½"
13½"

LAMP-ON FINGERBOARD

½" · 3"
6" | 2" | 5" | 1½"
14½"

AND-HELD FINGERBOARD

PROTECTION

WEAR FULL FACE SHIELD DURING LATHE TURNING, ROUTING, AND OTHER OPERATIONS THAT MAY THROW CHIPS

WEAR DUST MASK DURING SANDING AND SAWING

WEAR VAPOR MASK DURING FINISHING

WEAR SAFETY GLASSES OR GOGGLES AT ALL TIMES

WEAR RUBBER GLOVES FOR HANDLING DANGEROUS CHEMICALS

WEAR EAR PROTECTORS DURING ROUTING, PLANING, AND LONG, CONTINUOUS POWER TOOL OPERATION

THE WORKSHOP COMPANION™

WORKBENCHES AND SHOP FURNITURE

TECHNIQUES FOR BETTER WOODWORKING

by Nick Engler

Rodale Press
Emmaus, Pennsylvania

If you have any questions or comments concerning this book, please write:
Rodale Press
Book Readers' Service
33 East Minor Street
Emmaus, PA 18098

About the Author: Nick Engler is an experienced woodworker, writer, and teacher. He worked as a luthier for many years, making traditional American musical instruments before he founded *Hands On!* magazine. Today, he contributes to several woodworking magazines and teaches woodworking at the University of Cincinnati. He has written more than 30 books.

Series Editor: Jeff Day
Editors: Roger Yepsen
        Bob Moran
Copy Editor: Barbara Webb
Graphic Designer: Linda Watts
Graphic Artists: Mary Jane Favorite
              Chris Walendzak
Master Craftsman: Jim McCann
Photographer: Karen Callahan
Cover Photographer: Mitch Mandel
Proofreader: Hue Park
Indexer: Beverly Bremer
Typesetting by Computer Typography, Huber Heights, Ohio
Interior and endpaper illustrations by Mary Jane Favorite
Produced by Bookworks, Inc., West Milton, Ohio

Library of Congress Cataloging-in-Publication Data

Engler, Nick.
    Workbenches and shop furniture/by Nick Engler.
       p.   cm. — (The workshop companion)
    Includes index.
    ISBN 0–87596–579–2   hardcover
    1. Woodwork—Equipment and supplies—Design and
      construction. 2. Workshops—Equipment and sup-
      plies—Design and construction. 3. Workbenches—
      Design and construction. I. Title II. Series:
    Engler, Nick. Workshop companion.
    TT186.E53 1993
    684'.08'028—dc20   92–44580
                                  CIP

   6 8 10 9 7 5   hardcover

The author and editors who compiled this book have tried to make all the contents as accurate and as correct as possible. Plans, illustrations, photographs, and text have all been carefully checked and cross-checked. However, due to the variability of local conditions, construction materials, personal skill, and so on, neither the author nor Rodale Press assumes any responsibility for any injuries suffered, or for damages or other losses incurred that result from the material presented herein. All instructions and plans should be carefully studied and clearly understood before beginning construction.

Special Thanks to:

Larry Callahan
West Milton, Ohio

Carriage Hill Farm
Dayton-Montgomery County
  Park District
Dayton, Ohio

College of the Redwoods
Ft. Bragg, California

Garrett Wade, Inc.
New York, New York

Chester Hollins
Alpha, Ohio

Don Reuter
Columbus, Ohio

University of Cincinnati
Cincinnati, Ohio

Debbie Von Bokern
Cincinnati, Ohio

Wertz Hardware
West Milton, Ohio

Winterthur Museum
Winterthur, Delaware

Woodcraft
Parkersburg, West Virginia

CONTENTS

TECHNIQUES

PROJECTS

TECHNIQUES

1

ARRANGING SHOP FURNITURE

Ask a room full of woodworkers what's the best way to design a workbench or a tool cabinet, and no two will give you the same answer. The fact is, there is no clear answer. Many different styles and configurations will work, although some will work better than others. Furthermore, a design that works well for one woodworker may not work for another. Good, workable designs for the furnishings in your shop depend not only on their function, but also on:

- How you like to work
- What you like to build
- The available space

DESIGN CONSIDERATIONS

Despite the wide differences in the way we work, what we build, and the size of our shops, most woodworkers perform the same general tasks (sawing, sanding, drilling, etc.) and use the same types of tools and materials (hand tools, stationary tools, lumber, hardware, etc.). Consequently, when designing a new workbench or tool cabinet, most woodworkers have the same concerns: *supporting the work* and *organizing tools and materials*. For example, a workbench holds boards while you work on them and stores many of the tools you need to do the work. To a large extent, the design of the bench is determined by the kind of work you must support and the tools you must store. There are other considerations as well, just as important though not quite as apparent.

LEAVE ENOUGH SPACE TO WORK

All of the major fixtures in the shop — workbenches, tool cabinets, wood racks, stationary tools, and tool stands — occupy two different types of space. First of all, they take up *physical space,* which is determined by the actual dimensions of the item. And second, they require *working space,* which is the space that you need to work at a bench, open a cabinet, retrieve the wood from a rack, or use a tool. *(SEE FIGURE 1-1.)*

For example, to rip 8-foot-long boards on your table saw, there must be 8 feet of unobstructed space in front *and* in back of the saw — this is the working space that surrounds the saw. If the doors on a tool cabinet are 2 feet wide, you should leave at least 2 feet of working space in front of the cabinet to open it. If you want to mount both a tail vise and a face vise on your workbench, leave adequate working space on two adjacent sides of the bench to reach those vises. You should have not only enough physical space in your shop for a piece of furniture, but also enough working space *around* that fixture to use it properly. (See "Space Requirements for Common Shop Tools and Fixtures" on page 10.)

This is an extremely important (but often forgotten) requirement when designing shop furniture. You must consider the impact of a new fixture on the entire shop, especially the surrounding tools and benches. Can you make the new piece fit the space *and* leave enough space around it to maneuver the materials safely and easily? Will the addition of this piece crowd the working space required by other fixtures? If you simply add a new workbench or tool cabinet without considering the working space, you could find your-self constantly moving things in your shop just to get some work done. Or worse, you'll be tripping over your tools.

Oftentimes, the addition of a major fixture requires that you rearrange your shop to make better use of the space. When deciding where to locate the tools and benches, you can overlap the working spaces, but you should not place a fixture inside another's working space. To ensure that you allow enough working space, make a simple floor plan of your shop. Show both the physical space *and* the working space of existing tools and benches, as well as any planned additions.

Start by drawing a plan of the shop, showing the walls, windows, and doors to scale. You may also want to mark the locations of electrical outlets, ventilation fans, and other important features. On a separate piece of paper, draw the outlines of your stationary power tools, workbenches, and other major shop fixtures

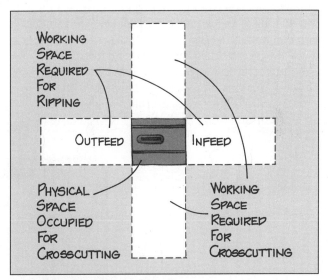

1-1 Shop furniture and power tools not only occupy *physical space* in your shop, they also require *working space*. There must be room around a bench or tool to maneuver materials and perform woodworking tasks. Some machines require different amounts of space for different tasks. For example, to rip a long board on a table saw, there must be unobstructed space on both the infeed and outfeed sides of the saw. To crosscut a board on the same tool, you need space to the right and left sides of the saw.

as seen from the top. Color or shade the areas inside each outline to represent the physical space occupied by the fixture. Then draw the working space that surrounds the item. Cut out the shapes of the working spaces. **Note:** You can also use different colors of paper to represent physical and working spaces.

Arrange the paper outlines on the floor plan of the shop. The unshaded areas — the working spaces — can overlap each other. This will still leave enough space around each tool and bench. However, the unshaded areas should not overlap the shaded ones — you cannot obstruct the working space of one tool by placing it too close to another. (*See Figure 1-2.*) Try to find an arrangement that leaves *all* the working spaces free and clear.

If you can't find an arrangement that accommodates the planned addition and provides enough working space, you still have several options. Remember that the working space has *height,* as well as length and breadth. You can place two fixtures close together as long as one rests below the working space of the other. For example, you can place a low jointer near a table saw. As long as the working space of the saw is higher than the jointer, the boards that you feed across the saw will pass over the shorter tool. (*See Figure 1-3.*)

You might also arrange tools and benches in "clusters," making one working space serve for all the items in a single cluster. To do this, you'll have to adjust the working space of all the items in a cluster to

TRY THIS TRICK

If you have a small shop, orient the table saw so the working space extends *diagonally* from corner to corner. This enables you to rip longer boards. The same trick also works for jointers and planers — any tool that requires a long, narrow working space.

WOOD STORAGE

DRILL PRESS

TABLE SAW

ROUTER TABLE

BAND SAW

WORKBENCH & TOOL CABINET

JOINTER

1-2 To determine the best arrangement of the stationary tools, workbenches, and other major fixtures in your workshop, you don't need an elaborate three-dimensional model — simply draw a floor plan and cut outlines of the tools *and* their working spaces from paper. To make sure you leave enough space around each tool, don't place the physical outline of a tool inside the working space of another. You can, however, overlap the working spaces.

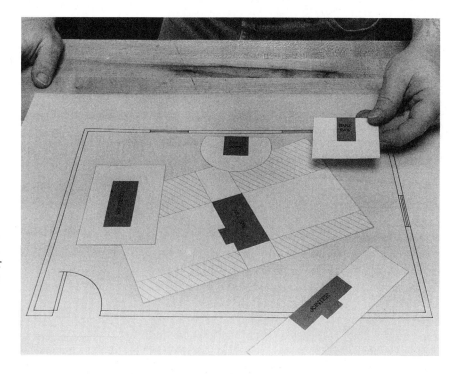

the same level, either by modifying the tool stands or by combining two or more tools on the same stand. (*SEE FIGURE 1-4.*) When the working spaces are flush with one another, you can work at any tool or bench in the cluster without the interference of nearby shop fixtures. Furthermore, you can use nearby work surfaces to help support large workpieces. This arrangement is particularly useful in a small shop.

1-3 If the working spaces of two fixtures are at different levels, you can sometimes place them side by side. For example, the working space of this band saw is well above the nearby router table. Any board you cut on the band saw will pass above the router table. And since the working space that surrounds the router table is smaller than that of the saw, the taller tool will not obstruct the work that is performed on the shorter one.

1-4 The craftsman who works in this small shop clustered the table saw, router table, and workbench in the center of the room. He combined the router table with the table saw extension, and raised the workbench until the benchtop was at the same level as the saw table. This allows him to use any one of the three fixtures without interference from the other two.

FOR YOUR INFORMATION

Some of the most useful and well-designed tool clusters are "multipurpose" stationary power tools, such as the Shopsmith, Robland, and Kity. Although some woodworkers are skeptical of these machines, many others have found them just as accurate and capable as traditional tools. If you have a small shop, they provide a good solution to the space problem. If you have a large shop, they are a space-efficient way to add tools that you use only occasionally. By carefully selecting accessories, you can configure these tools to serve many different functions. The multipurpose machine shown does quadruple duty as a dado cutter, lathe, disc sander, and scroll saw.

Finally, you can mount benches, cabinets, and tools on casters, making them *mobile*. This allows you to use the area in the center of your shop as a common working space for *all* your fixtures. Arrange the tools and benches that you need for a particular project or task in the center of the room, and store the remaining fixtures out of the way. This is an extremely versatile system. Not only can you fit more tools into a limited space, you can easily rearrange them to achieve a smooth work flow. The drawback is that you often have to move one fixture to work on another. You also have to provide *brakes* for the casters so your tools don't "walk" when you try to work on them. (For more on brakes and casters, see "Making Tools Mobile" on page 63.)

CREATE WORKSTATIONS

Workstations are items of shop furniture that keep related tools and accessories together, while supporting the workpiece. It makes sense to keep frequently used combinations of tools and accessories together in your shop. Workstations save time by keeping the tools needed for related tasks close at hand and easy to find. You work more efficiently and get more done, and your shop seems a more productive (and pleasant) place to be.

For example, you can design a stand for your drill press that will store the drill bits, or a cabinet for your radial arm saw that will hold the saw blades. If you use a hand-held router at the workbench, build a storage cupboard into the bench to hold the router. If it will save steps to keep the table saw, jointer, and planer together, combine them in a cluster. (*SEE FIGURES 1-5 AND 1-6.*)

KEEP OFTEN-USED ITEMS HANDY AND OCCASIONALLY USED ITEMS OUT OF THE WAY

Although the workstation system — keeping related tools and accessories together — makes sense, it doesn't always work when you have lots of related items. Consider the router workstation shown in *FIGURE 1-5*. The cabinet beneath the router table is not large enough to hold all the routing accessories that a well-equipped workshop might have. Instead, it's designed to hold just the *frequently* used routing tools, while the rest are stored elsewhere in the workshop. It takes a little longer to fetch them on the rare occasions that they're needed, but they're out of the way when you perform common routing chores.

You can make your woodworking a lot easier by keeping frequently used items handy. And just as important, you can eliminate clutter and free up working space simply by storing occasionally used items in out-of-the-way locations such as the corners of your workshop, closets, rafters, or another room. You may even want to design knock-down fixtures that can be easily disassembled and stored. (*SEE FIGURE 1-7.*)

You may wish to keep whole workstations out of the way if they aren't used frequently. For example, in my workshop I have a shaping and molding workstation — a small shaper mounted on a cabinet. This cabinet stores shaper cutters, a molding head, molder knives, and other related tools. The trouble is, the workstation takes up a lot of space and I don't use it more than once a week. So I've mounted it on wheels and keep it in a separate room. When I need to do some shaping or molding, I roll the entire workstation into the main workshop.

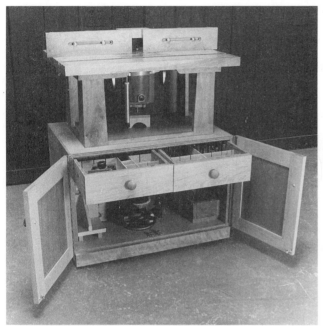

1-5 The router table and the
cabinet that it's mounted on form a
routing workstation. All the frequently used routing tools — hand-held
router, table-mounted router, router
bits, routing accessories — are stored
and used at the same location.

1-6 This rolling "clamp caddy"
stores many different types and sizes
of clamps, including hand screws,
bar clamps, C-clamps, and band
clamps. You can fetch the clamps a
few at a time from the clamp caddy,
or, if you need lots of clamps for a
particular job, you can move the cart
to wherever you're working to create
a mobile clamping workstation.

1-7 These sawhorses and
stretchers form a grid for cutting
plywood and other sheet materials.
Because this grid is used only occasionally, it's designed to be easily
knocked down and stored in a
corner.

MAKE YOUR SHOP FIXTURES SAFE AND COMFORTABLE

I've listed these two qualities — safety and comfort — together because a comfortable shop fixture *is* a safe shop fixture. When you have plenty of room to work and the work surface is at a comfortable height, then you can concentrate fully on the woodworking task at hand. You're less likely to become fatigued and make dangerous mistakes. Here are some specific suggestions to enhance your comfort and safety.

Build benches and tool stands so they hold work surfaces at a comfortable height. Commercial workbenches and tool stands are built to standard heights, widths, and depths, as shown in "Space Requirements for Common Shop Tools and Fixtures" on page 10. However, there are no standard woodworkers. By building your own shop furniture, you can adjust these fixtures to fit *you* and *your work*. For example, the tops of standard workbenches are 34 to 36 inches above the floor, but you may want to alter that if you're particularly tall or short. Similarly, the work surfaces of most router tables are 34 to 40 inches high. Woodworkers who rout mostly small pieces usually prefer their router tables higher; those who rout larger boards, lower. Use the standards as a jumping-off point, then adjust the dimensions to achieve the most comfortable configuration.

Make sure that tools and workbenches are adequately lit. Because so many home workshops are set up in basements, garages, and other areas without much lighting to begin with, they often are not well illuminated. There are many potentially dangerous operations performed in a workshop, so these rooms should be as well lighted as a surgical theater. If you need more light in your shop, consider building lights into tool stands and workbenches.

 A SAFETY REMINDER

Use a mixture of fluorescent *and* incandescent lights in your workshop. Fluorescent lights are more efficient, but they flicker faster than the eye can see. In some situations, this flicker may synchronize with a spinning blade or cutter, making it look like it's standing still. You may think the tool is turned off when it's not. An incandescent light or two will help prevent this dangerous optical illusion.

Provide convenient electrical service. You may want to install electrical outlets on workbenches, particularly if you use portable power tools at these locations. If your tool stands and workbenches are mobile, and you use the center of your workshop as a common working space, you may want to install floor outlets or overhead power drops. (*SEE FIGURE 1-8.*)

 A SAFETY REMINDER

Check that new electrical outlets and extension cords are rated to handle the load generated by your power tools. Powerful electrical motors often draw 20 amps or more. Also make sure the tools and the lights are on *separate* circuits. You don't want to be left in the dark should one of your tools overload a circuit in mid-cut.

1-8 **How do you keep from** tripping over electrical cords when using a power tool in the center of the workshop? Install *retractable electrical ceiling drops,* as shown. These special extension cords are available from many mail-order tool businesses, and you can purchase them from electrical supply stores. They are fairly expensive, but the safety and convenience make them well worth the money.

Collect as much dust as possible before it gets into the air. Not only is sawdust a nuisance, it can be a health hazard. It quickly fills the air in small shops and can irritate your skin, nose, throat, and lungs. It may also aggravate emphysema, asthma, and other respiratory ailments. To limit this hazard, install dust collectors on tool stands wherever possible. When arranging your shop, try to keep these collectors within reach of the shop vacuum so that you can easily hook them up and collect the dust as you work. (*See* Figure 1-9.)

A SAFETY REMINDER

Airborne dust is not only hard on you, it can harm your furnace and air conditioner. If your shop is heated or cooled with forced air, clean the filters *often*. If you use your shop daily, have a contractor install an air return with a two-stage filter to clean the air from your shop before it gets back to the furnace or central air conditioner.

1-9 Arrange the power tools that create the most sawdust close to the shop vacuum. Install dust collectors on the stands for these tools so you can vacuum the dust as you work. Here, three tools — a table saw, a jointer, and a planer — are hooked to the same shop vacuum. The "blast gates" near the outlet on the vacuum let you control the air flow in each hose.

ALLOW FOR CHANGE, BUT DON'T CHANGE NEEDLESSLY

Workshops constantly evolve as the woodworking skills and ambitions of the craftsmen who use them grow. Try to plan for these inevitable changes as you design your shop furniture. Make sure the benches, cabinets, and stands suit your personal needs, but design them to be as versatile as possible. Build them with adjustable shelves, movable drawer partitions, pegboards, and other storage devices that can be reconfigured as required. Think twice about installing built-in cabinets and other permanently installed fixtures — you will probably need to rearrange the fixtures in your workshop from time to time.

Carefully think through major additions to your shop, such as new stationary tools or tool cabinets. You may not have the luxury of adding more space or moving to a larger room. Instead, you'll have to make better or different use of the space that you have. You may also have to eliminate some major fixtures before you can add new ones.

This advice seems so obvious that it's hardly worth mentioning. Yet many people — even experienced craftsmen — let their workshops grow like weeds, acquiring woodworking tools until there's no room left for the woodworker. Ironically, many of these acquisitions may not be necessary or even beneficial. Some of us are such tool-aholics that we would rather make our shops less pleasant and less productive than pass up a tool sale!

Remember that the most precious commodity in most workshops is *space to work*. Before you purchase a new tool or build a piece of shop furniture, ask yourself whether the addition justifies the expense *and* the shop space. Is there some way you could accomplish the same tasks with the tools and furniture you already own? How will this change affect the work you do on *other* tools and benches? Will it restrict the work flow or interfere with foot traffic? Will it make some tools and materials less accessible? Any change should enhance the *whole* workshop, creating new opportunities for you to grow as a craftsman.

SPACE REQUIREMENTS FOR COMMON SHOP TOOLS AND FIXTURES

The workbenches, tool cabinets, and tool stands occupy two types of space in your workshop. First of all, they require *physical space* — that is, they take up room both horizontally and vertically. The horizontal room is determined by the length and width (or depth) of each fixture, while the vertical room is usually the height of the work surface. Sometimes these physical space requirements are fixed; sometimes they can be adjusted. For example, you can make a workbench whatever length and width you need. Or, you can change the height of a bench or tool by building the stand to hold the work surface at a comfortable level.

Second, shop fixtures require *working space*. You must have some unobstructed space around each tool or bench to feed the wood, maneuver the workpieces, or simply stand and work. Otherwise, you cannot work safely or efficiently.

Shown below are the physical outlines of common major shop fixtures and tools and the working space they require in most home workshops. The dimensions of both the physical and working spaces may change depending on the types of tools you own, the sorts of woodworking you do, and how you like to work, but the shapes will remain approximately the same.

LEGEND
—— Physical Space Requirement
------ Working Space Requirement

WORKBENCHES

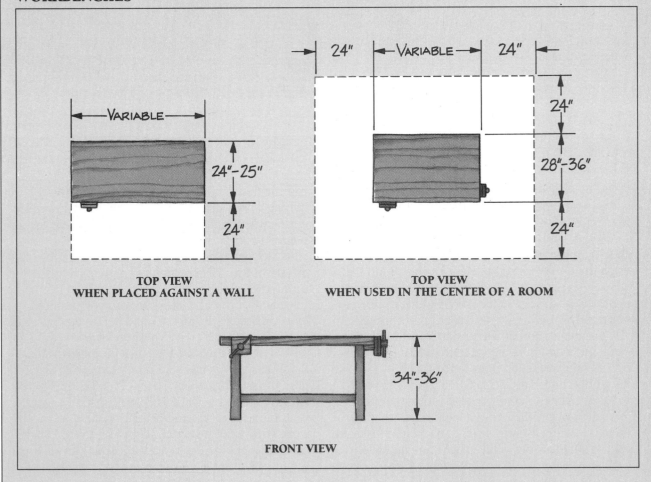

TOP VIEW
WHEN PLACED AGAINST A WALL

TOP VIEW
WHEN USED IN THE CENTER OF A ROOM

FRONT VIEW

TOOL CABINETS

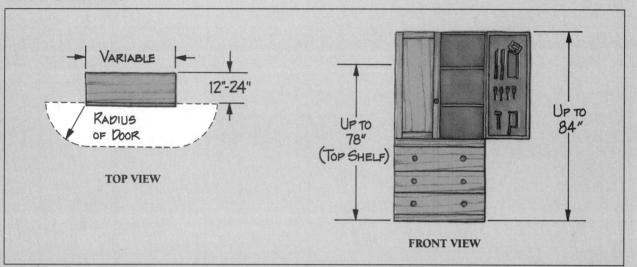

VARIABLE

12"-24"

RADIUS OF DOOR

TOP VIEW

UP TO 78" (TOP SHELF)

UP TO 84"

FRONT VIEW

TOOLS

SHAPER

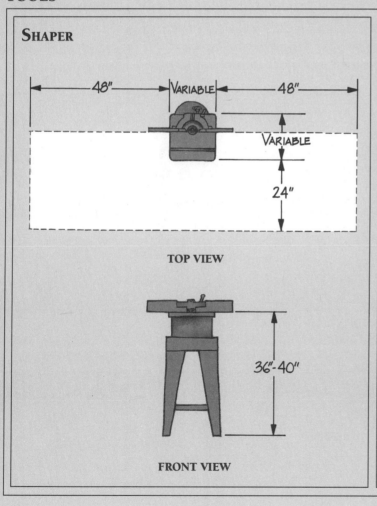

48" VARIABLE 48"

VARIABLE

24"

TOP VIEW

36"-40"

FRONT VIEW

DRILL PRESS

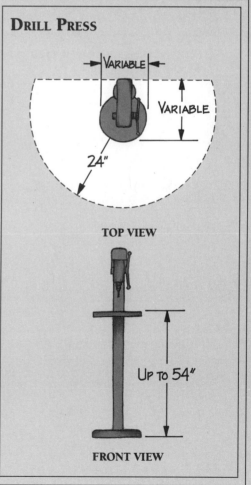

VARIABLE

VARIABLE

24"

TOP VIEW

UP TO 54"

FRONT VIEW

(continued) ▷

Space Requirements for Common Shop Tools and Fixtures — continued

TOOLS

Table Saw

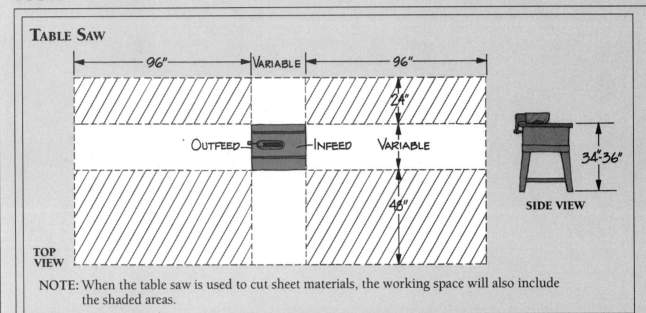

NOTE: When the table saw is used to cut sheet materials, the working space will also include the shaded areas.

Band Saw

NOTE: The band saw will require more working space on the infeed and outfeed sides if used for resawing.

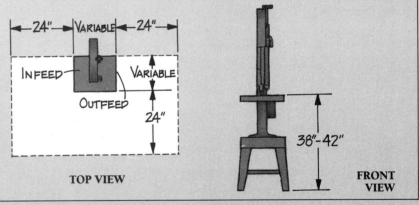

Planer

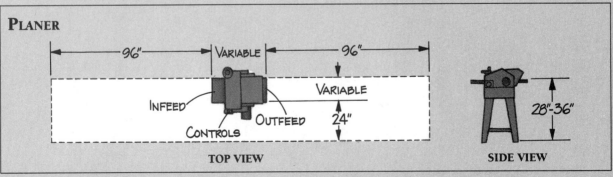

JOINTER

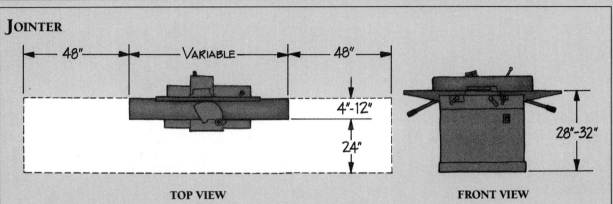

TOP VIEW **FRONT VIEW**

NOTE: On rare occasions, the jointer may require more working space on the infeed and outfeed ends.

LATHE

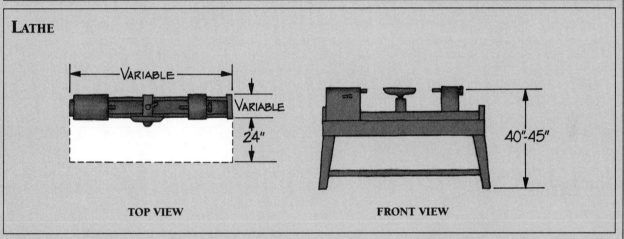

TOP VIEW **FRONT VIEW**

RADIAL ARM SAW

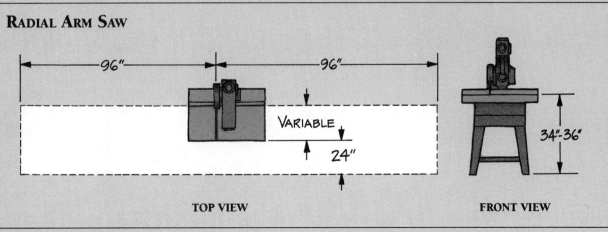

TOP VIEW **FRONT VIEW**

(continued) ▷

SPACE REQUIREMENTS FOR COMMON SHOP TOOLS AND FIXTURES — CONTINUED

TOOLS

ROUTER TABLE

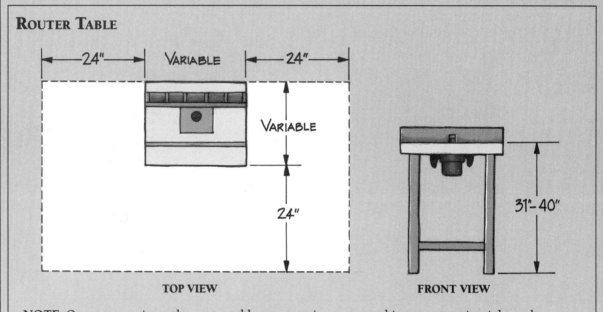

TOP VIEW   FRONT VIEW

NOTE: On rare occasions, the router table may require more working space on its right and left sides.

BELT SANDER/DISC SANDER

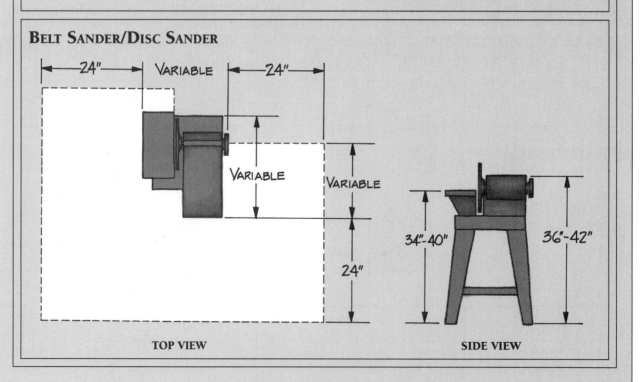

TOP VIEW   SIDE VIEW

2

WORKBENCHES

The heart of every workshop is its workbench. This is where all your woodworking ambitions are realized — you sketch plans, measure boards, join parts, sand surfaces, and apply finishes. Yet for all the activity that takes place on its surface, a workbench is a simple piece of furniture, one of the simplest in your shop.

Most benches are nothing more than a sturdy table with a vise or two. Many craftsmen customize their benches, sizing them to suit their work and adjusting the top to a comfortable working height. They may add holding devices or tool storage to aid their woodworking. But even the most sophisticated benches are, at their core, just a surface to work on.

A SHORT HISTORY OF WORKBENCHES

The workbench as we know it — a sturdy table that supports and holds the work — evolved with the hand plane. Without the simple workbench and its stops, the hand plane — one of the most important developments in the history of woodworking — would have been useless.

To hold the stock securely while they passed a plane across it, the Romans devised a low, flat table with a stop at one end. The Roman woodworker placed one end of a board against the stop, then planed toward the stop — the motion of the plane pressed the board against the stop, and the stop kept the board from scooting off the bench. (SEE FIGURE 2-1.) The Romans also may have used pegs, wedges, and L-shaped hold-downs to secure the wood to the bench-

top. To us, these devices seem rudimentary, but their significance cannot be overestimated.

The Dark Ages halted the development of woodworking, as they did so many other technologies. Neither the workbench nor any other woodworking tool improved much for over a thousand years. It wasn't until the fourteenth century, when a new interest in learning revitalized the arts and sciences, that woodworking tools and methods began to evolve again. Early in the Renaissance, European woodworkers started tinkering with the old Roman bench design. One of their first innovations was to cut a notch in the front edge. This served the same function as a vise — a craftsman placed a board in the notch, then secured it with a wedge. (SEE FIGURE 2-2.)

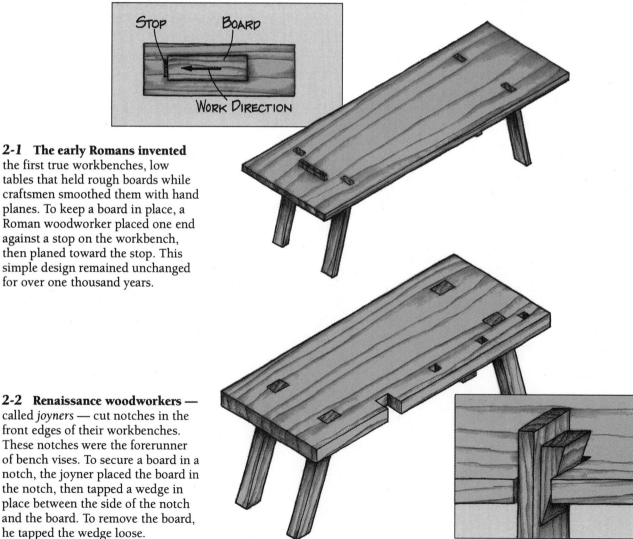

2-1 The early Romans invented the first true workbenches, low tables that held rough boards while craftsmen smoothed them with hand planes. To keep a board in place, a Roman woodworker placed one end against a stop on the workbench, then planed toward the stop. This simple design remained unchanged for over one thousand years.

2-2 Renaissance woodworkers — called *joyners* — cut notches in the front edges of their workbenches. These notches were the forerunner of bench vises. To secure a board in a notch, the joyner placed the board in the notch, then tapped a wedge in place between the side of the notch and the board. To remove the board, he tapped the wedge loose.

Woodworkers also developed *cleats* — L-shaped boards fastened to the front edge of the bench — to hold boards while they planed the edges. (*SEE FIGURE 2-3.*)

By the fifteenth century, craftsmen began to replace these notches and cleats with wooden *screw vises.* These worked in much the same way that vises do today — the woodworker turned a wooden screw to pinch a board between the movable jaw and the edge

of the bench. (*SEE FIGURE 2-4.*) At first, the vises were mounted only on the front edge of the workbench; later, they were also mounted on the ends of the bench. By the early eighteenth century, the classic "cabinet-maker's" workbench with two vises — one mounted on the front edge and another on an end — was widely used in Europe. (*SEE FIGURE 2-5.*)

2-3 Joyners also fastened L-shaped cleats to their benches, then wedged boards between the cleats and the front edges of the benchtops. These cleats functioned as both a stop and a vise. They were used to hold boards while the craftsmen planed and jointed the edges.

2-4 Perhaps the most important development in the evolution of the workbench was the invention of the *screw vise* around the end of the fifteenth century. These first vises were extremely simple, consisting of just a movable jaw, one or more screws, and nuts to fit them.

2-5 The European "cabinet- maker's" workbench — a bench with a vise mounted on the front edge and another mounted on an end — was in wide use by the beginning of the eighteenth century. This arrangement allowed the craftsman to hold different sizes of workpieces in several positions.

Originally, most workbenches were designed and built by the craftsman who used them. Then, in the nineteenth century, tool makers began to manufacture benches and offer them for sale. Some of these manufactured benches were highly mechanized, with all-metal vises and other special holding devices. Some were very ornate, with cast iron legs and stretchers in Victorian designs. But most of these mechanical contraptions and ornaments were passing fads. The most important improvement of the period was metal screws for vises — these proved to be much more durable and easier to operate than wooden screws.

Today's workbenches echo designs that have been used for hundreds of years. The major contribution of the twentieth century to workbench technology has been the materials used to make them. Benchtops are made not just from wood, but also from plywood, particleboard, hardboard, and plastic laminate. The legs can be wood, plastic, or metal. Contemporary benches also sport a variety of storage options, from a simple shelf underneath the benchtop to enclosed cupboards and drawers. But the basic design of the workbench — a sturdy surface with a means to hold the work — has remained unchanged.

WORKBENCH DESIGNS

Although there are many commercial workbenches available, many woodworkers still build their own, customizing the project to suit their own particular needs and aspirations. Because this piece of shop furniture is so highly personalized, there are tens of thousands of workbench designs and no recognized system of classification to help distinguish one from the other.

For the purpose of discussion, we have to borrow the classifications that have emerged for *manufactured* workbenches. Driven by a need to market these products, advertising copywriters have imposed a little order on workbench chaos. To encourage potential customers to make a choice, they have identified five broad categories of workbenches. Most of these bench types are distinguished by the number and the arrangement of vises.

Worktable — A worktable is simply a sturdy table on which you can work — a work surface on legs or a frame. (*SEE FIGURE 2-6.*) While it supports the work just as well as a more elaborate bench, the means for actually holding boards on the surface are very basic. You can nail a stop to the work surface or use a clamp to hold a board in place, but there are no vises, hold-downs, or other built-in devices for securing boards to the top. Despite this deficiency, worktables are useful for layout, finishing, and many other woodworking tasks that don't require you to fasten the work to the table.

Utility workbench — The simplest bench with a built-in holding device is a "utility" workbench (sometimes referred to as a "student" or "hobbyist" workbench in catalogs). This is just a table with a single

2-6 A *worktable* is the most basic type of bench — it provides work space, but no vises, bench dogs, hold-downs, or similar holding devices. Many workbenches start out as simple worktables, then become more elaborate as the craftsman adds various means to hold the work.

vise mounted on the front or side. (*See Figure 2-7.*) It's a modest design but very capable. For many home workshop owners, there's nothing to be gained by building anything more grandiose. After all, how many vises can you use at one time?

Cabinetmaker's workbench — This is the classic workbench that first appeared in the eighteenth century, and it has changed little since then. It normally has two vises, a *face vise* mounted on the front edge and a *tail vise* mounted on an end, although other types of vises can be used. (*See Figure 2-8.*) It has a single row of holes for bench dogs along the front edge, which are used in conjunction with the tail vise. In addition, there is sometimes a tool bin along the back.

Carver's workbench — The name of this workbench is something of a misnomer, since it's not designed especially for woodcarving, but for many woodworking tasks. The feature that distinguishes it from a classic cabinetmaker's bench is a second row of holes for bench dogs along the back edge — this increases the

2-7 A *utility workbench* has a work surface and a single vise. Most workbenches are a variation of this simple but capable design. You can increase the usefulness of the bench by choosing a vise with a *pop-up dog* — a small jaw face that can be raised above the vise. When used in conjunction with bench dogs, this arrangement extends the capacity of the vise.

2-8 A modern *cabinetmaker's workbench* normally has a face vise mounted on the front edge and a tail vise mounted on an end. Both have a similar capacity — typically, the movable jaws of a vise open as far as 6 to 12 inches. However, the tail vise works in conjunction with bench dogs, which are mounted in the movable jaw *and* along the length of the bench. Consequently, the tail vise will hold boards almost as long as the bench itself.

holding capacity. (SEE FIGURE 2-9.) Instead of a tail vise, there is usually a wide face vise or two separate face vises mounted on one end. The tool bin, if there is one, may be mounted opposite the end vise.

Specialty workbenches — In addition to traditional table-like benches, there are many specially designed workbenches for various woodworking tasks. Some of these are recent developments; others are the products of centuries of tradition. For example:

■ Old-time chairmakers, boat builders, coopers, and many other woodworking tradesmen used variations

of the *shaving horse*. (SEE FIGURE 2-10.) These horses provide a small work surface, a foot-operated clamp, and a comfortable place to sit and work.

2-9 A *carver's workbench* has two rows of bench dog holes, one along the front edge and another along the back edge. This allows you to use the entire surface of the workbench as a giant clamp. Although the name implies that the bench would be best suited for holding small workpieces for woodcarving, it is, in fact, designed to hold large ones for all sorts of woodworking tasks. *Photo of Versatile Style Workbench courtesy of Garrett Wade Co., New York, N.Y.*

2-10 A traditional *shaving horse* provides a craftsman with a place to sit and work. A foot pedal operates the "dumbhead," pressing it down against the work surface. To hold the work in place, position the board between the dumbhead and the work surface, then push the foot pedal forward. To release it, simply release the foot pressure.

■ Many country craftsmen depended on the *brake,* a simple device that holds a workpiece steady by wedging it between two sticks. Contemporary brakes are useful for holding small parts while you work on them. (*SEE FIGURE 2-11.*)

■ Woodcarvers work on many shapes and styles of benches, some custom-designed to hold a particular type of carving. One of their favorites is a *carving pedestal,* which allows easy access to all sides of the carving. (*SEE FIGURE 2-12.*)

2-11 A brake is perhaps the simplest of all workbenches. Both the work surface and the board to be worked on are placed between two sticks or crossbars. The downward pressure of the work pinches the board between the work surface and the upper stick. Here, the side of a small box is held in place while it's shaped and sanded.

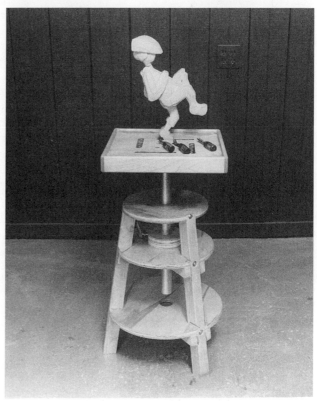

2-12 Many carvers prefer to mount their work on a small *carving pedestal* rather than a larger work-bench. The pedestal lets them walk around the work so they can reach all sides and carve from any angle. The work is secured to the pedestal with a bench screw.

■ Japanese woodworkers rely on a unique *beam and trestle* to hold the wood for planing. (*SEE FIGURE 2-13.*) The work rests against a stop on the angled beam as the craftsman *pulls* (rather than pushes) the plane along the wood.

■ Thousands of home craftsmen rely on the *Workmate* to provide a work surface for every conceivable do-it-yourself project. This ingenious device converts to become a small workbench, sawhorse, step stool, vise, and hold-down. (*SEE FIGURE 2-14.*)

2-13 When the plane was introduced to Japanese woodworkers in the fifteenth century, they developed a unique apparatus to hold the wood while they planed it. One end of a thick beam is propped up on a trestle so it rests at an angle. Toward the low end, a stop is fastened. To use this *beam and trestle,* you place a board on the beam with one end against the stop. Starting at the high end, pull the plane down along the board.

2-14 Ron Hickman, a South African automotive designer-turned-inventor, developed the versatile *Workmate* in the late 1960s, and Black & Decker began to manufacture it in 1972. This small, portable workbench will hold many different sizes and shapes of boards at almost any comfortable working height. The unique split top serves as both a work surface and a vise.

WORKBENCH CONSTRUCTION

Just as there are different workbench designs, there are different ways to build each design. Most workbenches have three separate components — benchtop, frame, and tool storage. For each component, you can choose various materials, methods of construction, and other options.

MAKING THE BENCHTOP

The earliest work surfaces for workbenches were just wide, flat beams. The oldest workbench still in existence is a Roman-style bench found in Saalburg, Germany, and dated about 250 B.C. All that's left is its top, a single oak plank 2¾ inches thick, 14½ inches wide, and 102 inches long. Massive hardwood beams such as these were an obvious choice because they were sturdy, inexpensive, and easy to replace. Traditionally, woodworkers set these beams with the heartwood (the inside of the tree) facing up because it made a harder work surface.

As sawmills became commonplace, woodworkers assembled benchtops from several planks. The best benchtops were laminated strips of hardwood — what we call *butcherblock tops* today. In a butcherblock, the "grain planes" of each strip are oriented so the assembled top is as hard and stable as possible. There are three of these planes in a board — the *longitudinal* plane, which runs parallel to the wood grain; the *radial* plane, which radiates out from the center of the tree through the annual rings; and the *tangential* plane, which runs tangent to the annual rings. Wood is fairly stable along the longitudinal plane, but it expands and contracts across both the radial and tangential planes. Furthermore, most species expand *twice* as much tangentially as radially. So the individual strips in a butcherblock present the radial plane to the surface. (*SEE FIGURE 2-15.*) This keeps the expansion and contraction to a minimum. Also, the radial plane has more compressive strength, making it more durable than the tangential plane.

Today, most lumber is "plain sawn" so the tangential plane runs across the width of the boards. To make your own butcherblock benchtop, rip hardwood boards into strips, turn them on edge, and glue them face to face. (Some craftsmen suggest bolting the strips together with long threaded rods, but with today's durable glues, this isn't necessary.) The traditional woods for butcherblocks are maple, beech, and oak, but you can use any clear hardwood.

Several twentieth-century building materials make good benchtops. (*SEE FIGURE 2-16.*) Shop-grade *plywood*, for instance, is extremely stable and, as long as it has a hardwood core, is fairly durable.

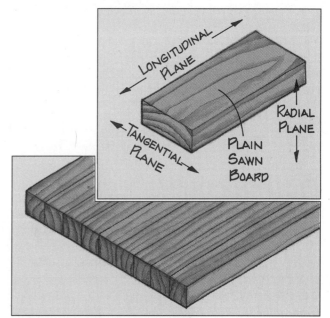

2-15 Butcherblock tops are made from strips of hardwood, laminated face to face. Each strip is turned so the annual rings run vertically, presenting the radial plane to the surface. Since the radial plane has more compressive strength, and wood expands and contracts less across the radial plane than it does across the tangential plane, this arrangement keeps the top as hard and as stable as possible.

2-16 In addition to traditional hardwood benchtops, there are many modern construction materials that you can use to make a durable benchtop. Shown are four common choices: a *softwood butcherblock* (1) made from clear two-by-fours, shop grade *plywood* (2) edged with hardwood, *particleboard* covered with *tempered hardboard* (3), and *particleboard* covered with *plastic laminate* (4).

Particleboard makes an acceptable benchtop, especially when it's covered with *tempered hardboard.* Don't glue the hardboard to the particleboard. Just tack it in place with brads, setting the heads of the brads slightly below the surface so they don't scratch your work. The particleboard provides the mass and strength you need, while the hardboard provides a smooth surface. Like plywood, a particleboard/hardboard sandwich is very stable, and as long as it rests on a level framework, it will remain flat. It isn't as durable as hardwood or plywood, but you can easily replace the tacked-down hardboard as it becomes stained and worn.

In some cases, you may wish to use particleboard covered with *plastic laminate.* Laminate is too hard and brittle for a general-purpose benchtop, but it makes a great work surface for a gluing bench or a finishing bench since it's impervious to most chemicals. It's also a good choice if you plan to slide boards across the surface, since laminate generates less friction than other materials. For example, if you mount a router under the workbench so it will do double duty as a router table, you may want to cover the surface with laminate. Or, if the bench is clustered with a table saw, and you occasionally use the surface to support large workpieces while you saw them, then laminate is a good idea.

FOR BEST RESULTS

If you make your benchtop from hardwood, softwood, plywood, or a particleboard/hardboard sandwich, apply a durable finish such as tung oil, spar varnish, or polyurethane. (If you've used an open-grain wood such as oak, fill the wood grain before applying the finish.) Then — no matter *what* material you've used — thoroughly wax and buff the work surface. Apply a new layer of wax and buff it out every six months or so. The wax will prevent glue from sticking and spilled chemicals from soaking into the benchtop.

MAKING THE FRAME

Over the centuries, craftsmen have developed dozens of ways to support benchtops, from tree trunks to saw-horses to cast iron supports to plastic legs. The three most common methods are legs and stretchers, trestles, and cabinets. (SEE FIGURE 2-17.)

Legs and stretchers — The earliest workbenches rested on four stout legs mortised into the benchtop. Gradually, this assembly method gave way to modern table construction, in which bench legs are joined with aprons and stretchers to make them more rigid. Instead of the ends of the legs being mortised into the underside of the top, the aprons are joined to the benchtops with cleats or pocket screws.

Trestles — A trestle is a frame with two uprights and two crossbars, usually joined with mortises and tenons.

The benchtop rests on two or more trestles, which are often joined with stretchers for added strength. The lower crossbar of each trestle serves as a foot, while the upper crossbar attaches to the underside of the benchtop, braces it, and helps keep it level. One advantage of this particular construction method is that it's easily disassembled, should you need to store the workbench or replace a component.

Cabinets — Instead of using a wooden framework to support the top, you can rest it on a plywood case, much like a modern kitchen counter rests on a cabinet unit. This plywood case not only holds up the benchtop, it also provides storage for tools. Use 3/4-inch plywood for the sides *and* back of the case to make sure it's plenty sturdy.

2-17 Shown are three common construction methods used to support a workbench top at a comfortable working height. *Legs and stretchers* (1) are similar to contemporary table joinery — the legs are joined with aprons and stretchers, then the aprons are joined to the benchtop. *Trestles* (2) are simple frames that can be easily attached to (or detached from) the underside of a benchtop. *Cabinets* (3) are sturdy plywood cases on which a benchtop rests. These cases also provide storage for tools.

ADDING TOOL STORAGE

Until a few hundred years ago, tool storage wasn't an important consideration in workbench design. The few tools that most old-time woodworkers owned could usually be kept in a simple chest. However, today even modestly equipped craftsmen would be hard-pressed to shoehorn all their tools into a chest. Consequently, many woodworkers make use of the space beneath their workbench to store their favorite tools (SEE FIGURE 2-18):

Open shelves — This is the simplest type of workbench storage. Just stretch a few boards between the legs or the stretchers, and rest tools on them. The tools are easy to find and easy to reach. The drawback is that open shelves collect dust, and the tools and materials stored on them may become covered with it.

Cupboards — The shelves in cupboards are enclosed by a wooden case. One or more sides of the case have doors, so you can easily reach the objects on the shelves inside. A cupboard requires more materials and more time to build than open shelves, but it protects the tools stored in it from dust.

Drawers — Like cupboards, drawers store *and* protect the tools. They also provide easy access. Because you reach into a cupboard from the side, you

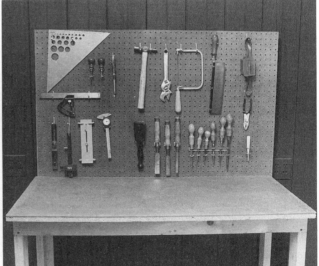

2-18 Here are several ways to store tools and materials under your workbench: The workbench at the upper left has two large *open shelves* and two *drawers* under the work surface, and a *fixed bin* attached to the work surface. The bench on the upper right has a single open shelf and several drawers, as well as several enclosed *cupboards.* You can hang tools by attaching a *pegboard* to the bench, as shown on the bottom right. Or, install hooks, racks, and *pegs* beneath the work surface, as shown on the bottom left. Organize small items by building *portable bins* for shelves and drawers, also shown on the bottom left.

often have to move items on the near side of the shelf to reach a tool on the far side. Drawers, however, are accessed from the top, so you don't have to move things (as long as the drawers aren't too deep).

Bins — There are two types of tool bins: fixed and portable. Fixed bins are built into benchtops or are attached to the edges. These bins keep small tools and materials handy but *below the work surface,* where they might be in the way of the work. Portable bins are small, open-top boxes that rest on shelves or in drawers. The advantage to portable bins is that you can remove them from the bench and carry the contents to wherever you are working. They are particularly handy for storing small items such as scrapers, drill bits, or screws.

Pegs, hooks, and racks — There are many common storage devices that allow you to hang small tools from the vertical surfaces of your workbench. For example, you might install a wooden peg in the front leg to keep a bench brush handy. Or, screw a cup hook into the side of a workbench cabinet to hang a straightedge. Or, fasten a rack to the edge of the benchtop to store a set of chisels.

Pegboard — One of the most versatile workshop storage devices is the pegboard, a piece of hardboard with evenly spaced holes all over the surface. There are dozens of commercial pegs, hooks, and racks that are specially designed to fit in these holes, allowing you to place them wherever you need them on the pegboard. Many woodworkers mount pegboards on the walls behind their workbenches to hold oft-used tools. You can also mount pegboard to cabinet sides and doors.

Try This Trick

Place a small *camphor* tablet in enclosed spaces — cupboards, drawers, and bins — to keep the contents from rusting. Camphor evaporates very slowly (an individual tablet will last several months), giving off fumes that coat metal surfaces with a thin, oily film. This film provides a barrier to moisture and prevents rust. Camphor tablets are available at most drugstores.

WORKBENCH OPTIONS

Shown here and on the next page are common design options for shop-made workbenches. Mix and match these components, choosing one option for the work surface, another for the frame, and as many options for tool storage as you need, to create the best possible workbench for your shop.

WORK SURFACE

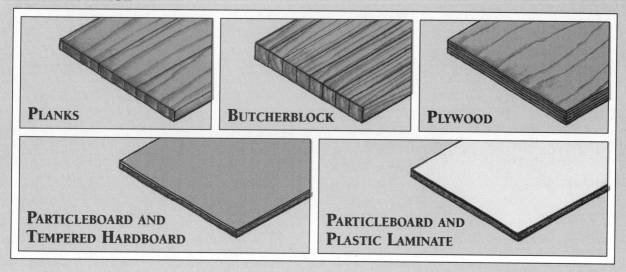

PLANKS

BUTCHERBLOCK

PLYWOOD

PARTICLEBOARD AND TEMPERED HARDBOARD

PARTICLEBOARD AND PLASTIC LAMINATE

(continued) ▷

WORKBENCH OPTIONS — CONTINUED

FRAMEWORK

LEGS AND STRETCHERS
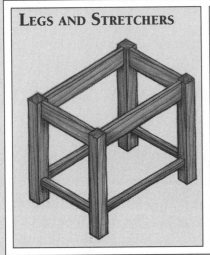

TRESTLES

CABINET
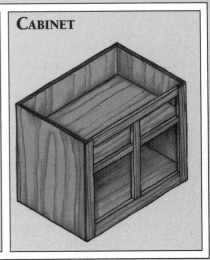

TOOL STORAGE

CUPBOARDS
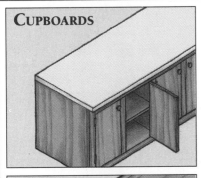

DRAWERS
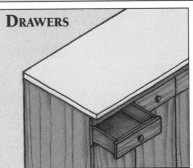

OPEN SHELVES
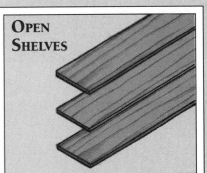

BINS
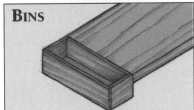

RACKS

PEGBOARD
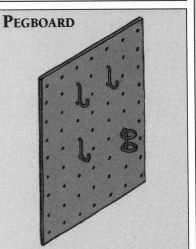

PEGS
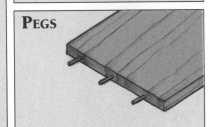

HOOKS
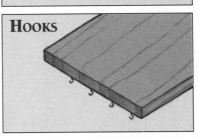

3

VISES AND
WORKBENCH ACCESSORIES

The feature that distinguishes a workbench from an ordinary work table is that a workbench doesn't just support the work, but *holds* it as well. And the device that normally does the holding is a *vise*. There are many types of vises, from the ordinary face vise, with a single wooden jaw that moves in and out, to the all-metal patternmaker's vise, with multiple jaws that swivel, tilt, and rotate. A workbench may have two or more kinds of vises, plus other accessories for securing the workpiece.

Stops and dogs, for example, keep the work from sliding around on the benchtop. Brakes and holdfasts press the work down on the bench. Bench hooks secure boards face up; bench slaves support boards edge up.

TYPES OF VISES

An old woodworker's pun goes, "You can't have too many vises." That's true in a large professional shop, perhaps, but most home workshops can get along well with just one or two. The trick is to choose a vise with sufficient capacity and versatility to handle the type of woodworking you like to do.

All vises have two things in common:

■ A *movable jaw* that pinches the work against a fixed jaw or the edge of the benchtop

■ A long threaded shaft or *screw* to move the movable jaw back and forth

In addition, most vises have a *handle* to turn the screw, a threaded *nut* to fit the screw, and a *collar* through which the screw passes. The nut is fixed, while the collar is movable. There may also be a *fixed jaw* opposite the movable jaw, *guide rods* or *guide plates* to keep the movable jaw aligned as it moves back and forth, and a *mounting plate* to fasten the vise to the workbench. (*SEE FIGURE 3-1.*) Beyond these similarities, however, there are considerable differences in the design and function of vises and their various parts.

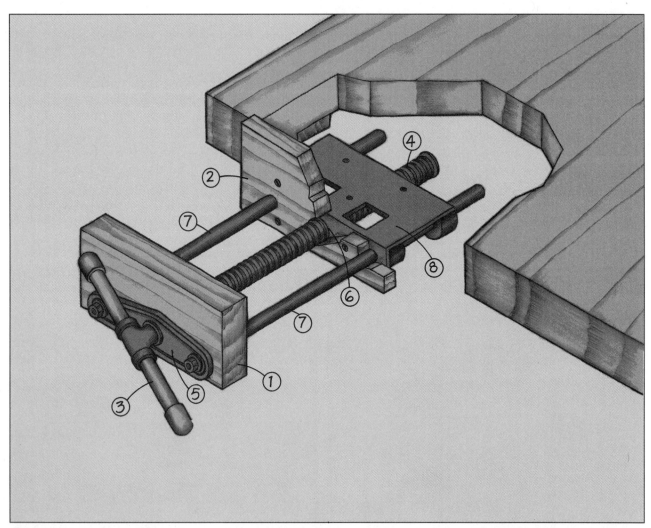

3-1 A typical woodworking vise has one *movable jaw* (1), which clamps the work against either the edge of the benchtop or a *fixed jaw* (2). To open or close the jaws, you turn the *handle* (3). This spins a large *screw* (4), which passes through a *collar* (5) and a *nut* (6). The collar is fastened to the movable jaw, while the nut is fastened to the fixed jaw or is part of the mounting plate. As the screw turns in the nut, the collar drives the movable jaw in or out. *Guide rods* (7) keep the movable jaw aligned with the fixed jaw as the vise opens and closes. A *mounting plate* (8) secures the entire assembly to the workbench.

FOR YOUR INFORMATION

The jaws of most vises are angled slightly to meet at the top first. Because the screw is usually positioned below the jaws and there is always some slop or clearance in the mechanism, the moving jaw will tilt slightly as you tighten it. The pressure spreads evenly across the jaws, and the entire holding surface of the vise contacts the workpiece. On the other hand, if the jaws were perfectly parallel to begin with, they would gap at the top when the vise was tightened — only the bottom portion of the jaw faces would hold the workpiece.

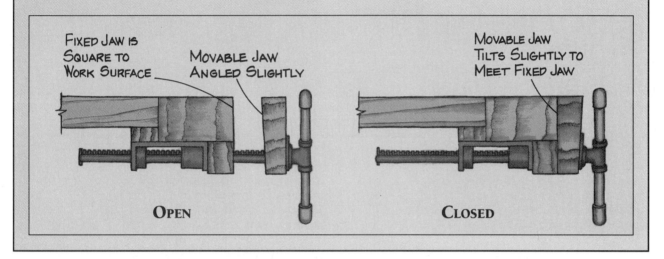

FIXED JAW IS SQUARE TO WORK SURFACE

MOVABLE JAW ANGLED SLIGHTLY

MOVABLE JAW TILTS SLIGHTLY TO MEET FIXED JAW

OPEN

CLOSED

COMMON WOODWORKING VISES

There are five common types of vises:

A *face vise* is the simplest of all vises, and one of the most versatile. It mounts on the edge or end of the benchtop and has one wooden face that moves out from or in toward the bench. Usually, this vise has just one metal screw, although face vises with unusually long jaws may have two. (*See Figure 3-2.*)

A *shoulder vise* is designed to secure boards with their edges facing up, although it will hold them in other positions as well. This device evolved from the L-shaped cleats that medieval joyners once fastened to the front edges of their workbenches. (*See Figure 2-3* on page 17.) In the sixteenth century, when screw vises became the preferred method for holding work to a workbench, joyners drove a screw through the cleat and added a movable jaw. This created a vise with a positive stop for planing the edges of boards. (*See Figure 3-3.*)

Just as the shoulder vise developed to hold boards edge up, the *tail vise* developed to hold boards face up. The movable portion of this vise is a large wooden block that mounts on the front corner of a workbench. There are *dog holes* — mortises for bench dogs — along the front edge of the workbench *and* in the movable block. By inserting one dog in the movable block and another in the benchtop, you can hold long boards and large assemblies on the workbench. (*See Figures 3-4 and 3-5.*)

3-2 A *face vise* has a single wooden jaw that moves in and out. The work is held between the jaw face and the edge of the benchtop.

3-3 Craftsmen who like to work with hand planes often prefer a *shoulder vise* to a face vise on the front of their workbenches. The shoulder of this L-shaped vise provides a positive stop when planing the edges of boards.

3-4 A *tail vise* has a much larger capacity than any other common vise. It consists of a long, movable wooden block mounted on the front corner of the workbench. Both the movable block and the benchtop are mortised for bench dogs. By inserting one dog in the block and another in the bench, you can secure a workpiece almost as long as the bench itself.

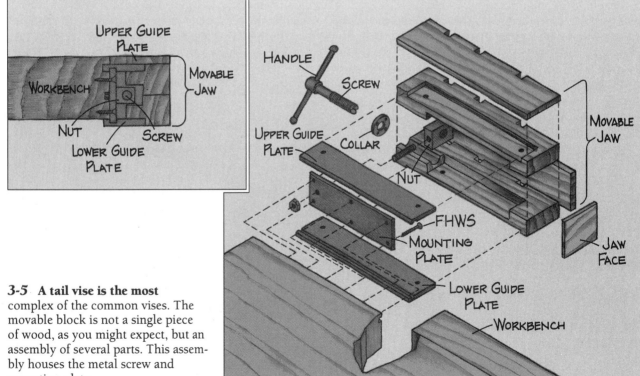

3-5 A tail vise is the most complex of the common vises. The movable block is not a single piece of wood, as you might expect, but an assembly of several parts. This assembly houses the metal screw and mounting plate.

FOR YOUR INFORMATION

Most cabinetmakers' workbenches combine a face vise for small and medium-size work and a tail vise for large workpieces. However, some craftsmen prefer to mount a shoulder vise instead of a face vise. When used with a tail vise, this combination lets them mount boards edge up or face up, whichever is needed.

On a *leg vise*, the jaws are much taller than they are wide. The movable jaw pivots at the bottom end as it moves back and forth. In some cases, the movable jaw is hinged to a long, horizontal bar that slides in and out of the workbench leg. This increases the capacity of the vise — to hold larger pieces, you slide the bar (with the movable jaw attached) out from the leg. (*SEE FIGURE 3-6.*)

On a *bench vise,* both the screw *and* the jaws are made from metal. Since their introduction in the nineteenth century, these all-metal devices have become the most common type of woodworking vise. They owe their popularity to their durability and versatility, and the ease with which they can be installed — they can be mounted on most workbenches with a few carriage bolts or lag screws. Their only disadvantage is that the metal jaws must be faced with wood to avoid marring the work. (*SEE FIGURE 3-7.*)

3-6 A *leg vise* has a long, vertical jaw that pivots at the bottom end. The pivot is often attached to a horizontal bar that slides in and out of the workbench leg. This arrangement eliminates the need for guide rods and makes it easy to extend the capacity of the vise. It's one of the easiest and most economical vises to make — all you need to purchase is a single bench screw. And although the jaws are not as long as a face vise, it's just as versatile.

3-7 The most popular type of woodworking vise is the *bench vise*. This all-metal vise is durable, versatile, and easy to mount. Its nominal capacity is comparable to that of a face vise, but many have a *pop-up dog* in the movable face. When used with bench dogs, the working capacity can be as long or as wide as the workbench itself.

CUSTOMIZING A BENCH VISE

A common bench vise is fairly versatile, but you can make it even more so with the addition of custom-made jaws, jaw faces, and vise mounts. Here are several simple-to-make options that will enable you to hold odd-shaped boards at different angles.

1 **Before mounting the wooden** jaw faces to the bench vise, clamp the faces together and bore several holes through the *width* of the stock where the boards join. When you take the boards apart, these holes should form two matching sets of round-bottom grooves. Use these grooves to hold dowels and odd-shaped stock vertically. You may also wish to cut V-grooves through the *length* of each jaw near the top edge, using a table saw or a router. These will hold stock horizontally.

2 **After making the grooved** jaw faces, cut a block of wood in a triangular shape with two acute corners (less than 90 degrees) and one obtuse corner (more than 90 degrees). Attach a dowel to the obtuse corner. This dowel must be the same diameter as one of the vertical grooves in the jaw faces. When you place the dowel in a groove on the movable face, the triangular block becomes a swiveling jaw for holding tapered and other odd-shaped workpieces.

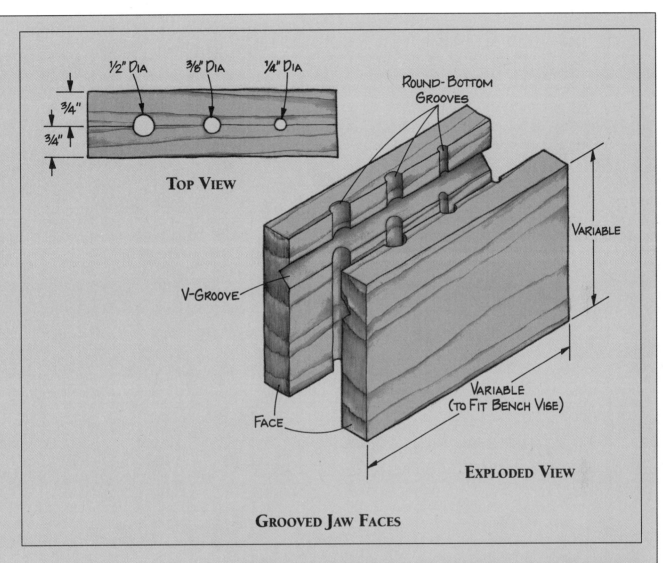

½" DIA   ⅜" DIA   ¼" DIA

¾"

¾"

TOP VIEW

ROUND-BOTTOM
GROOVES

VARIABLE

V-GROOVE

VARIABLE
(TO FIT BENCH VISE)

FACE

EXPLODED VIEW

GROOVED JAW FACES

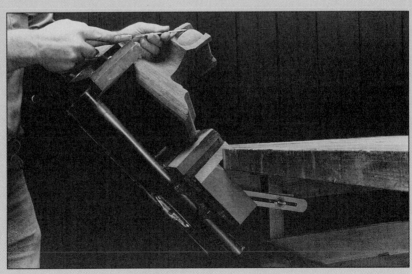

3 **By mounting a vise to a** hinged mount, you can tilt the jaws from horizontal to vertical. This mount is L-shaped and has a pivoting arm attached to one side to hold the vise at the desired angle. Install a hanger bolt in the leg of your workbench and fit the groove in the arm over the bolt. Secure the arm to the leg with a flat washer and a wing nut.

(continued) ▷

CUSTOMIZING A BENCH VISE — CONTINUED

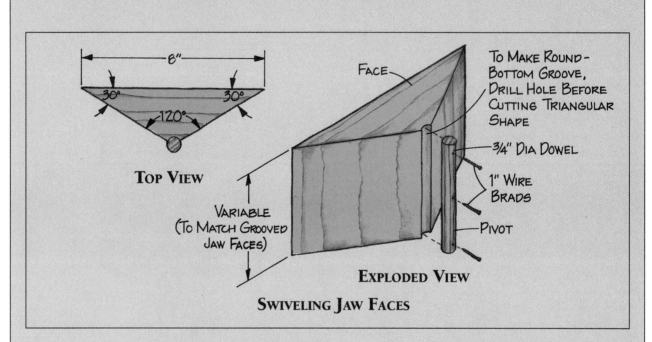

8"

30°   30°
120°

TOP VIEW

FACE

TO MAKE ROUND-
BOTTOM GROOVE,
DRILL HOLE BEFORE
CUTTING TRIANGULAR
SHAPE

3/4" DIA DOWEL

1" WIRE
BRADS

PIVOT

VARIABLE
(TO MATCH GROOVED
JAW FACES)

EXPLODED VIEW

SWIVELING JAW FACES

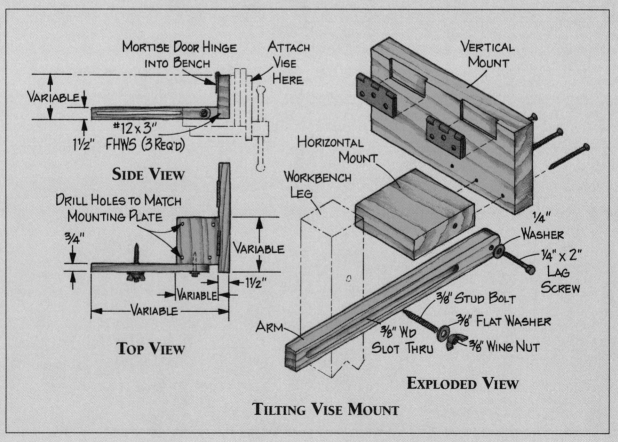

MORTISE DOOR HINGE
INTO BENCH

ATTACH
VISE
HERE

VARIABLE

1 1/2"

#12 x 3"
FHWS (3 REQ'D)

SIDE VIEW

DRILL HOLES TO MATCH
MOUNTING PLATE

3/4"

VARIABLE

VARIABLE

1 1/2"

VARIABLE

TOP VIEW

VERTICAL
MOUNT

HORIZONTAL
MOUNT

WORKBENCH
LEG

1/4"
WASHER

1/4" x 2"
LAG
SCREW

3/8" STUD BOLT

3/8" FLAT WASHER

3/8" WING NUT

3/8" WD
SLOT THRU

ARM

EXPLODED VIEW

TILTING VISE MOUNT

SPECIALTY VISES

Many vises are designed for specific tasks or types of work.

A *mechanic's vise* is intended for general metalworking. This all-metal vise mounts on the *top* of the workbench, rather than the bench edge like most woodworking vises. It isn't well suited to woodworking tasks since the jaw faces are metal and will mar the work. However, it is a handy vise for sharpening, tool repair, and occasional metal cutting, soldering, welding, or grinding. (SEE FIGURE 3-8.) **Note:** In some tool catalogs, mechanic's vises are also referred to as bench vises.

3-8 A *mechanic's vise* is designed for metalworking. It's made completely from metal, mounts on the top of the workbench, and holds the work well above the bench surface. The bases of most mechanic's vises swivel, allowing you to approach the work from any side.

Like a mechanic's vise, a *carver's vise* mounts on the top of a workbench and holds the work above the work surface, but there the similarity ends. The jaw faces of a carver's vise are either made of softwood or lined with rubber to keep from marring the wood. In addition, the jaws of a carver's vise can be tilted to many different angles, and the base rotates in a full circle. This allows the carver to hold the work in almost any position. (SEE FIGURE 3-9.)

A *gunstock vise* also mounts on the benchtop and looks similar to a carver's vise. But instead of the jaws tilting, they *swivel* to accommodate different shapes. This vise also rotates 360 degrees so you can approach the work from any angle. These vises are extremely useful for exacting work such as doweling, intricate joinery, marquetry, and inlay. (SEE FIGURE 3-10.)

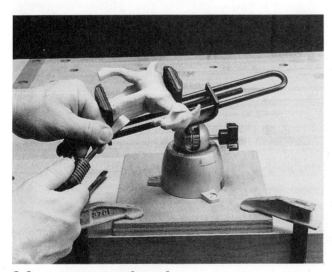

3-9 A *carver's vise* tilts and rotates to hold the work at almost any angle. These vises are used primarily to hold small and medium-size workpieces; most don't have the capacity or the strength to hold large carving projects.

3-10 A *gunstock vise* has jaws that swivel to accommodate different shapes, and a rotating base so the work can be turned in a complete circle. The capacity of these vises is usually limited to 6 or 7 inches, but they are useful when you must hold small or narrow, odd-shaped pieces.

TRY THIS TRICK

If you own a mechanic's, carver's, or gunstock vise and only use it once in a while, mount it on a small scrap of plywood and attach a cleat to the bottom face of the plywood, flush with the front edge. When you need the vise, hold the cleat in the jaws of a vise that's permanently mounted to the workbench. Or, clamp the plywood to the bench-top with the cleat overhanging the edge. When you're not using the vise, remove it and store it out of the way.

At first glance, a *patternmaker's vise* looks much like a bench vise. However, patternmakers routinely work with boards of all shapes and sizes, which they assemble to make accurate and exacting assemblies of all descriptions. To accommodate this diverse, meticulous work, a patternmaker's vise has a larger capacity than even the largest bench vises. The jaws tilt and swivel to hold a variety of shapes, and the entire vise rotates to hold the work at almost any angle. Some had a second set of jaws to hold the work above the bench.

Perhaps the most widely acclaimed patternmaker's vise was the Emmert Universal Roto-Vise, which was manufactured from the late nineteenth century until 1965. (SEE FIGURE 3-11.) Many craftsmen considered this to be the ultimate woodworking vise not only because of its versatility, but also because it was relatively easy to set up and use. Today, Veritas Tools, Inc., markets the *Tucker Vise,* which looks very similar to the old Emmert and incorporates many of its features. (SEE FIGURE 3-12.)

3-11 Many craftsmen consider the *patternmaker's vise* to be the most versatile of all woodworking vises. It has a large capacity, pop-up dogs, and jaws that tilt, swivel, *and* rotate. The vise shown was once the Cadillac of patternmaker's vises, the Emmert Universal Roto-Vise. It was manufactured during the first half of the twentieth century. Today, Emmert vises can bring over one thousand dollars at tool auctions!

3-12 Although Veritas Tools, Inc., does not market its *Tucker Vise* as a patternmaker's vise, it looks and functions much like the old Emmert vises. Its inventor, engineer Ed Tucker, also included several additional features and improvements, such as cork-lined jaw faces to keep from marring the work and a quick-release mechanism to easily position the movable jaw. The Tucker Vise is available through several mail-order tool suppliers.

Stops, Dogs, and Hold-Downs

In addition to vises, there are several other devices you might add to your workbench to help hold the work. For example, a *stop* butts against the edge of a board to keep it from shifting on the benchtop. A *dog* works in the same manner, but it's movable and is used in conjunction with a vise. Finally, a *hold-down* presses the board down onto the benchtop.

WORKBENCH STOPS

A stop is just a strip of wood fastened to the surface of your workbench. To use it, simply place the workpiece on the bench with an end or edge against the stop, and plan your work so the action of the tool forces the board against the stop. For some operations, you may want to wedge the board between two stops.

Here are three common stops you can make yourself:

■ A *right-angle stop* consists of two strips of wood scewed or nailed to the workbench at right angles to one another. This holds a corner of a board, keeping it more stable than a single strip. (SEE FIGURE 3-13.) Furthermore, you don't have to work in just one direction; the tool can travel in any direction within a 90-degree arc.

■ A *movable stop* can be inserted into two dog holes in the benchtop. (SEE FIGURE 3-14.) It can be moved wherever there are dog holes to mount it, and you can remove the stop and store it out of the way.

■ A *pop-up stop* is usually fastened to the end of the bench with hanger bolts and wing nuts. (SEE FIGURE 3-15.) The stop has vertical slots, allowing you to position it above the work surface when you need a stop, and below the surface when you don't.

3-13 A *right-angle stop* consists of two strips of wood fastened to the benchtop to form a right angle. This arrangement holds two adjoining surfaces of a board rather than just a single surface.

3-14 A *movable stop* consists of a strip of wood with a dowel attached to each end. The dowels fit the dog holes in the benchtop, allowing you to arrange the stop in several different positions on the work surface or remove it completely.

3-15 A *pop-up stop* is permanently attached to the workbench, but it can be positioned above or below the work surface as needed. This particular stop is mounted inside the tool bin near the end of the workbench.

BENCH DOGS

A bench dog is similar to a stop — it holds the edge or the end of a board. However, there are two important differences:

■ Dogs are used in conjunction with vises. They are, in fact, small jaw faces that extend the capacity of a vise.

■ Dogs are always movable. They mount in holes in the benchtop and in the movable jaws of vises so they can be positioned wherever they're needed. This allows you to increase the vise capacity a few inches or a few feet, as required.

When using bench dogs in conjunction with a face or tail vise, mount the dogs in the benchtop *and* in the movable jaw of the vise. Many bench vises have their own built-in dog, eliminating the need to mount bench dogs in the vise jaw. However, if you have a bench vise without a built-in dog and you want to use bench dogs with it, fasten a thick wooden face to the movable jaw. Mortise or bore holes in this face for bench dogs.

Bench dogs can be either round or square and may be made of metal or wood. *(SEE FIGURES 3-16 AND 3-17.)* Each shape and material has its advantages. Square dogs are more stable, but round dogs can be turned to accommodate odd-shaped workpieces. Wooden dogs will not mar the work, but metal dogs are more durable. Shop-made dogs are ordinarily made from wood; commercially made dogs are usually metal. Most woodworkers who make their own workbenches find it

3-17 Some bench dogs are designed for specific tasks. The metal dog shown has a small, built-in screw clamp — this is useful when joining complex assemblies on your benchtop. The wooden dog has a face with a V-shaped notch in one side, used to assemble frames.

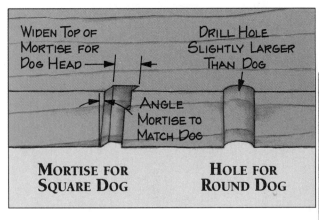

3-16 Bench dogs are small, movable jaw faces that mount in the benchtop and extend the capacity of the vises. They may be round or square, made of metal or wood. Square dogs are mounted in mortises, while round dogs fit in holes.

WIDEN TOP OF MORTISE FOR DOG HEAD →

DRILL HOLE SLIGHTLY LARGER THAN DOG

ANGLE MORTISE TO MATCH DOG

MORTISE FOR SQUARE DOG

HOLE FOR ROUND DOG

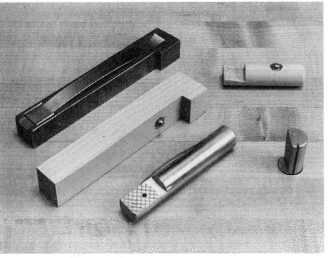

easier to make round dogs because it's less trouble to drill holes than it is to cut mortises.

Bench dogs often have springs that press against the side of the hole or mortise. The friction from the side spring lets you position the dog at different heights above the work surface. When you don't need the dogs, push them down into the dog holes so the heads are below the work surface.

FOR YOUR INFORMATION

When making your own bench dogs, or cutting mortises for commercial dogs, do not make the faces perfectly square to the benchtop. They must angle *down* 2 or 3 degrees. This slightly acute angle helps hold the workpieces against the benchtop.

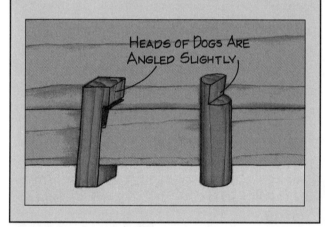

HEADS OF DOGS ARE ANGLED SLIGHTLY

BENCH HOLD-DOWNS

Unlike stops and dogs, hold-downs do not grasp the edge or ends of a board. Instead, they press down on the *face* of the board, pinching it between the hold-down and the surface of the bench.

■ Perhaps the simplest type of hold-down is the *holdfast* or *pinch dog*. This is a thick, round iron shaft with a long arm or "beak" protruding sideways from one end. The shaft mounts in a hole in the benchtop, while the arm extends over the board. (SEE FIGURE 3-18.) When you hit the top of the shaft with a hammer, this sets the holdfast in its hole and the arm presses down on the board.

■ On a *screw holdfast*, the arm pivots at the end of the shaft and a screw moves the arm up or down. (SEE FIGURE 3-19.) This device has two advantages over a simple holdfast. You don't need a hammer to set it, and the pressure applied by the arm is much easier to control.

3-18 The *holdfast* consists of a metal shaft with an arm extending from one end. To use a holdfast, insert the shaft in a hole in the workbench and position the arm to lie across a board. Then whack the top of the holdfast (where the arm joins the shaft) with a mallet. This drives the shaft deeper into the hole, and the arm springs slightly to pinch the board and hold it to the bench. To release the holdfast, whack the *side* of the shaft with a mallet.

3-19 The *screw holdfast* evolved from the common L-shaped holdfast. Like its ancestor, it fits in a hole in the workbench and secures the work under an arm. However, it works like a vise. To hold a board down on the workbench, turn a screw at the top of the holdfast. As you advance this screw, the arm moves down and presses against the board.

■ A *rope brake* is a small, bench-mounted version of an old-time cleaving brake. A long wooden beam or paddle, attached to a rope and a foot treadle, holds the work down on the benchtop. *(SEE FIGURE 3-20.)*

■ *Go-bars* are supple wooden poles, cut just a little longer than the distance between the benchtop and the ceiling of the workshop. By bending the poles slightly to fit between the ceiling and a board on the workbench, you can generate enough spring tension to secure the board to the benchtop. *(SEE FIGURE 3-21.)* **Note:** Depending on your shop, you may have to screw a plywood plate to the ceiling above the workbench to prevent the go-bars from poking holes in the plaster.

3-20 A *rope brake* uses a long wooden paddle to hold the work down on a workbench. The shaft of this paddle is attached to a rope, and the rope is threaded through a bench dog hole. The other end of the rope is fastened to a foot treadle. To use the brake, place a board under the paddle and step on the treadle. This pulls the brake down, holding the board to the work surface.

3-21 A *go-bar* or *spring pole* is a long, slender stick, supple enough to bend easily and resilient enough to spring back. To use a go-bar, brace the top end against the workshop ceiling, bend the pole slightly, and position the bottom end over the work. When you release the go-bar, the spring tension in the pole will hold the work to the benchtop.

SHOP-MADE STOPS, DOGS, AND HOLD-DOWNS

Stops, dogs, and hold-downs are, next to vises, the most useful workbench accessories you can own. They are also easy to make. Here are several simple designs.

1 **This *adjustable stop* mounts** in the bench dog holes in a workbench. You can adjust the position of the mounting dowels to change the placement of the stop on the workbench as needed. In addition, you can insert pegs in the edge of the stop to hold the corners of workpieces and keep them from sliding along the stop.

2 **These *wooden bench dogs* are** similar to many commercially made dogs, except that they use bullet catches in place of the usual side springs. These catches provide the friction needed to hold the stops at the desired height above the work surface.

(continued) ▷

SHOP-MADE STOPS, DOGS, AND HOLD-DOWNS — CONTINUED

3 These *screw go-bars* use carriage bolts and T-nuts to hold a workpiece down on the workbench, rather than relying on the spring tension generated by bending the bars. The top ends of the bars butt against a U-shaped frame that clamps to the workbench. Some craftsmen prefer to build a *go-bar box* instead of a frame. The advantage of a box is that you can mount go-bars at many different locations on the work, along not only the length but also the width. This is useful when gluing up complex assemblies, applying veneer, doing marquetry, and carrying out many other operations where you need to apply pressure over a broad area.

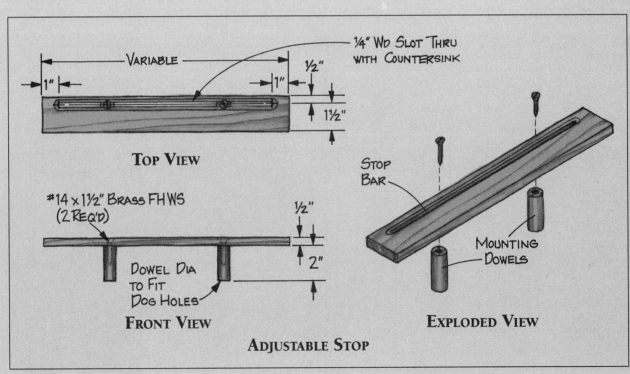

VARIABLE

1"

¼" WD SLOT THRU WITH COUNTERSINK

½"

1"

1½"

TOP VIEW

#14 x 1½" BRASS FH WS (2 REQ'D)

½"

2"

DOWEL DIA TO FIT DOG HOLES

FRONT VIEW

STOP BAR

MOUNTING DOWELS

EXPLODED VIEW

ADJUSTABLE STOP

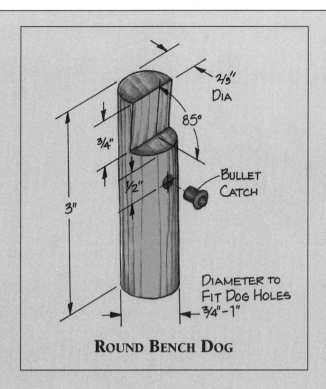

ROUND BENCH DOG

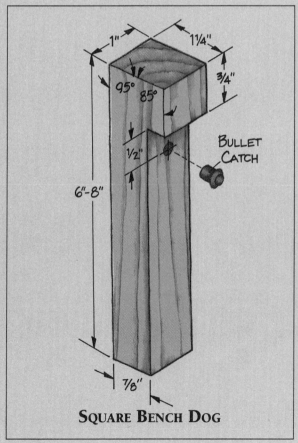

SQUARE BENCH DOG

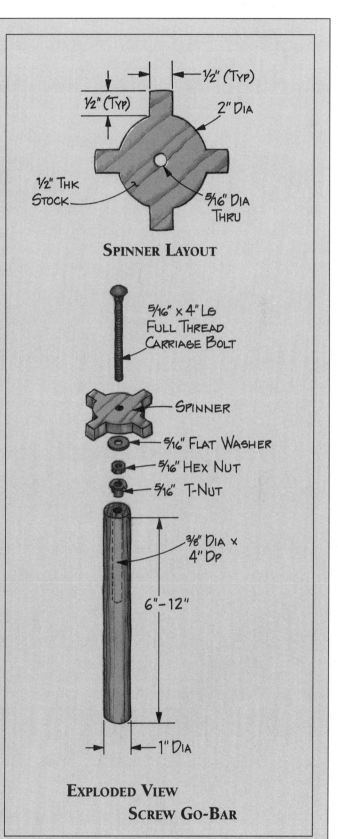

SPINNER LAYOUT

EXPLODED VIEW
SCREW GO-BAR

(continued) ▷

SHOP-MADE STOPS, DOGS, AND HOLD-DOWNS — CONTINUED

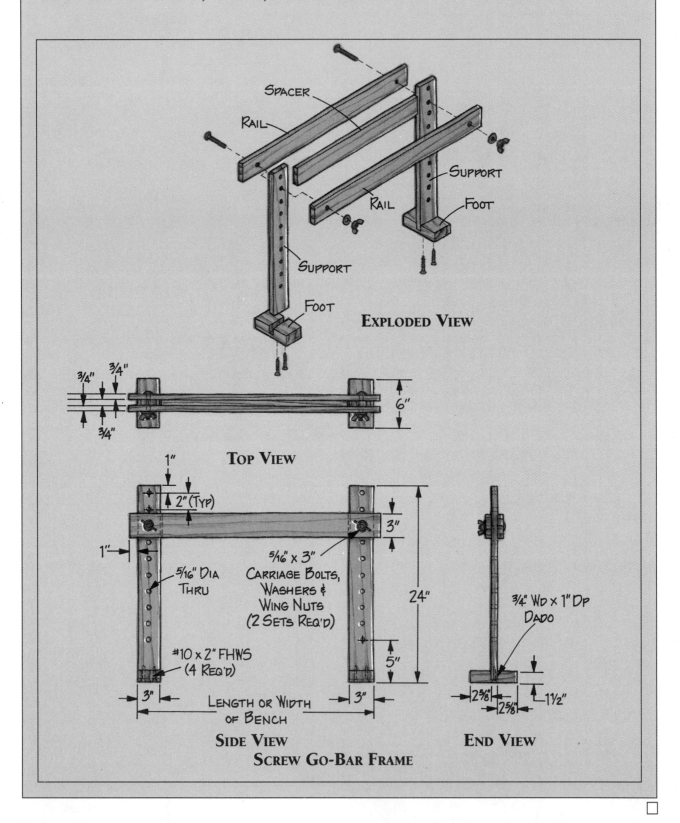

SPACER

RAIL

SUPPORT

RAIL

SUPPORT

FOOT

FOOT

EXPLODED VIEW

3/4" 3/4"

3/4"

6"

TOP VIEW

1"

2" (TYP)

3"

1"

5/16" DIA
THRU

5/16" x 3"
CARRIAGE BOLTS,
WASHERS &
WING NUTS
(2 SETS REQ'D)

24"

5"

#10 x 2" FHWS
(4 REQ'D)

3/4" WD x 1" DP
DADO

3"

LENGTH OR WIDTH
OF BENCH

3"

2 5/8"

2 5/8"

1 1/2"

SIDE VIEW   **END VIEW**

SCREW GO-BAR FRAME

OTHER WORKBENCH ACCESSORIES

In addition to vises, stops, dogs, and hold-downs, there are several other workbench accessories that help hold the work.

A *bench hook* is a simple S-shaped jig that hooks over the edge of your workbench. It holds boards and protects the benchtop when cutting to length. *(SEE FIGURE 3-22.)* **Note:** Most bench hooks are designed to work with standard European saws — saws that cut on the *push* stroke. To work with Japanese saws, which cut on the *pull* stroke, they must hook over the *back* edge of the workbench.

A *shooting board* guides a hand plane to trim the end or edge of a board. *(SEE FIGURE 3-23.)* This is especially useful when fitting joints.

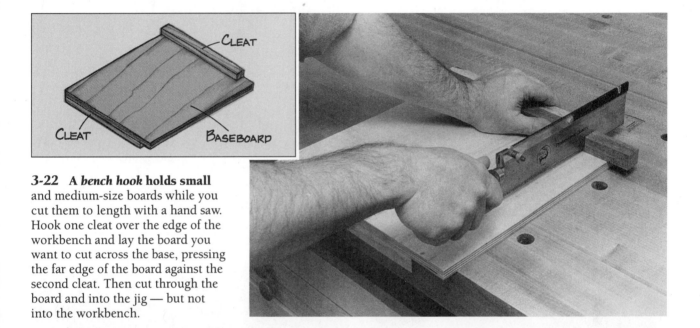

3-22 A *bench hook* holds small and medium-size boards while you cut them to length with a hand saw. Hook one cleat over the edge of the workbench and lay the board you want to cut across the base, pressing the far edge of the board against the second cleat. Then cut through the board and into the jig — but not into the workbench.

3-23 A *shooting board* is used with a hand plane to trim or true boards. There are many different designs, but they all have a fence attached to the baseboard to guide the hand plane. To use a shooting board, hook it over the benchtop and lay a board across it with an edge or end against a cleat. Place the sole of a hand plane against the fence and pass the plane across the board.

A *bench slave* (also called a bench jack) supports one end of a long board. It's normally used in conjunction with a vise. Clamp one end of the board in the vise, then adjust the bench slave to support the other end. (SEE FIGURE 3-24.)

Although a *tool bin* is ordinarily considered a storage device rather than a holding device, it can be designed for double duty. By making the bottom of the bin removable, you can use it as a "sawing well" to support workpieces when using a saber saw, coping saw, or similar cutting tool. (SEE FIGURE 3-25.)

A *clamping grid* is made of wood strips, joined so both the top and bottom surfaces of the strips are flush. This jig comes in handy when assembling odd-shaped parts that would otherwise be difficult to clamp together. Instead of pinching the parts between the jaws of the clamps, clamp each part to the grid and let the grid hold them together until the glue dries. (SEE FIGURE 3-26.)

3-24 A bench slave supports the free end of a board or assembly while the other end is clamped in a vise. This jig is particularly handy when you want to hold a long board on edge.

3-25 A tool bin is useful not only for storing small tools and materials, but also as a sawing well. Place the board you want to saw across the bin so it's supported on both sides, then make the cut over the bin opening. Note that the bottom of this bin is removable to accommodate long sawblades — and so it won't collect sawdust.

3-26 For some odd-ball assemblies, it's easier to clamp the parts to a *clamping grid* while the glue dries than it is to try to clamp the parts together directly. Clamping grids also allow you to attach clamps to the centers and interiors of assemblies. Some clamping grids are detached accessories, while others are built into the tops of workbenches.

4

Tool Stands

When woodworkers set out to reorganize or improve their workshops, they often overlook the tool stands. Few of us are satisfied with the austere, workaday stands provided by most power tool manufacturers, but we focus our attention on more obvious deficiencies in our shops. Ironically, these tool stands are usually the fixtures that are most in need of improvement or replacement.

Consider this: When manufacturers must cut costs, they are more likely to make cheaper stands than reduce the quality of the tools themselves. They know that the design of the stand rarely enters into your decision whether or not to buy the tool — you're more interested in how the tool works than what it rests on. Consequently, you get stuck with a cheap stand that does little more than prop up the tool. The space underneath the tool is often completely wasted.

If you take the time to replace these stands with sturdy storage units, you can reclaim an enormous amount of space in your shop. You will improve efficiency and work flow by keeping your power tool accessories under the tools themselves. The tools can be made safer and more enjoyable to use by building the new stands to hold them at a more comfortable height. And in many cases, these homemade stands will prove stronger and steadier than the commercial stands they replace.

DESIGNING A STORAGE STAND

Storage stands are specially constructed both to support power tools and to add storage space. They have to be a good deal more substantial than ordinary storage furniture, such as kitchen cupboards or bookshelves. A stand must bear the weight of both the tool and the work that has to be done on it. This, in fact, is your most important consideration when designing a storage stand — it should be at least as sturdy as the commercial stand it replaces.

STRUCTURE

To support a tool weighing two or three hundred pounds *and* provide storage space, you can rely on the legs, trestles, and cabinets used in workbench construction. (See "Making the Frame" on page 25.) If you use legs or trestles, you must hang open shelves or an enclosed cupboard between them to provide storage. If you build a cabinet, you must beef up the construction to provide sufficient support.

Perhaps the most versatile storage stand structure (and the simplest to build) is a *box*. Surprisingly, an ordinary wooden box will support all but the heaviest power tools, provided that you make it from sufficiently strong materials, brace it well, and join it properly.

4-1 A box-type storage stand looks like a cabinet, but it's much stronger and simpler to build. To make the stand sturdy enough to support a heavy power tool, cut the structural (weight-bearing) parts from plywood or hardwood that's *at least* ¾ inch thick. On the stand shown, for example, the top, bottom, sides, fixed shelf, divider, and braces are all made from shop-grade ¾-inch birch plywood or 4/4 (four-quarters) maple. Only the door panels and drawer bottoms are made from thinner materials.

Materials — When making a box-type storage stand, use shop-grade plywood and dense hardwoods such as oak or maple. When comparing equal weights, these materials are *stronger than steel!* Use nothing thinner than ¾-inch-thick stock for the top, bottom, sides, and any inside parts that help to reinforce the shell, such as fixed shelves or dividers. (*See Figure 4-1.*)

Bracework — Add braces to those parts that must bear the most weight, particularly the top of the box. Otherwise, these parts may bow. (*See Figure 4-2.*)

Joinery — Don't butt together the major structural parts (those parts that must bear most of the weight); use fitted joints to increase the gluing area and add strength to the box. This joinery doesn't have to be complex — simple rabbets, dadoes, and grooves will do. (*See Figures 4-3 and 4-4.*)

In addition to being simple to build, boxes are also simple to outfit with shelves, doors, and drawers. To mount shelves in a box-constructed storage stand, you can fit them in dadoes, attach them with cleats, or rest them on pins. (*See Figure 4-5.*) Doors can overlay the front edges of the box, and you can use almost any type of hinge to hang them. (*See Figure 4-6.*) Drawers can rest on fixed shelves; there's no need to build complex web frames and drawer guides. Or, you can hang them on wooden rails, drawer brackets, or extension slides. (*See Figure 4-7.*)

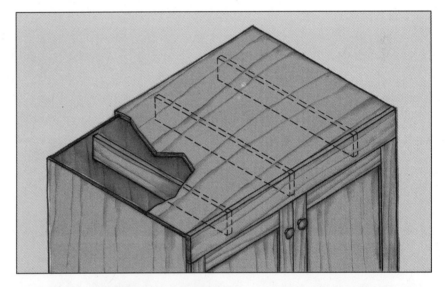

4-2 The top of the stand is braced to support the weight of the tool. These braces are evenly spaced boards that run horizontally under the top, like the joists under a floor. **Note:** For maximum strength, braces should always span the *shortest* possible distance. In some stands, this will be the distance between the front and back, as shown. In other stands, it may be the distance between the sides or between a divider and the sides.

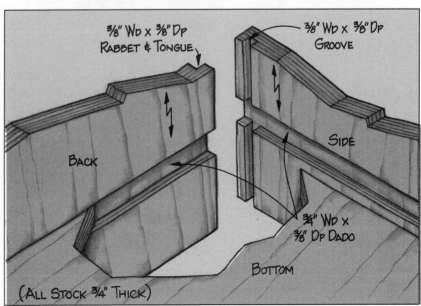

4-3 For maximum strength, the structural parts should interlock, not just butt together. Here is one possible joinery system for the back rear corner of a storage stand. All the joints are simple rabbets, dadoes, or grooves.

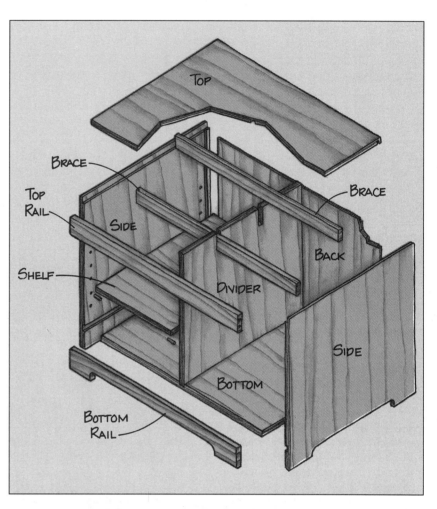

4-4 Arrange the structural parts to reinforce one another. On this design for a storage stand, the top and sides support most of the weight. The bottom prevents the sides from splaying out, while the back keeps the structure square. The braces and the divider strengthen the top and keep it from bowing. All the pieces work together to make an extremely strong structure. And yet this structure is mostly hollow, with plenty of room inside for storage.

4-5 To mount shelves in a box-constructed storage stand, cut dadoes in the sides to hold them; or, tack cleats to the sides and rest the shelves on them. You can also drill vertical rows of holes in the sides, insert shelving support pins in the holes, then rest the shelves on the pins. This pin system makes the shelves *adjustable* — if you want to change the height of the shelves, simply move the pins up or down.

4-6 When hanging doors on a box-constructed stand, attach them directly to the sides — you don't have to build a face frame. You can use almost any type of hinge, but European-style hinges are perhaps the simplest to mount because you can adjust them in all three directions. If you plan to hang accessories on the doors, mount them on piano hinges — these are designed to support more weight than other types of hinges.

4-7 There are several simple ways to mount drawers in box-constructed stands. For one or two drawers, the easiest method is to rest them on fixed shelves. However, fixed shelves require lots of materials and waste space inside a stand. When mounting several drawers, it's more economical to hang them from hardwood rails — attach the rails to the sides of the stand, then cut grooves in the drawer sides to fit the rails.

OVERALL SIZE AND SHAPE

When you have decided on a suitable structure, give some thought to the size and shape of the stand. First, consider its "footprint" — the length and width. If space is precious in your workshop, you probably won't want to make the stand much longer or wider than the tool itself. In most cases, this will probably work just fine, but there are some circumstances when you might want to make the footprint of the stand larger than that of the tool:

■ If the tool is much taller than it is long or wide, a stand with a small footprint might make it top heavy. This is true especially for drill presses and band saws, which tend to tip over if mounted on small stands. (*SEE FIGURE 4-8.*)

■ Should the motor, speed changer, or dust collector for the tool take up additional room on the stand, you will have to make the stand larger than the tool. (*SEE FIGURE 4-9.*)

■ Certain accessories for power tools may be larger than the tools themselves. Or, there may be too many accessories to fit in a stand that's only as large as the tool itself. In either case, you may want to make the stand with enough space to accommodate this equipment. (*SEE FIGURE 4-10.*)

Also give careful thought to the stand's height. The height of a tool's work surface, more than any other dimension, determines how comfortable that tool is to work on. If you are shorter or taller than average,

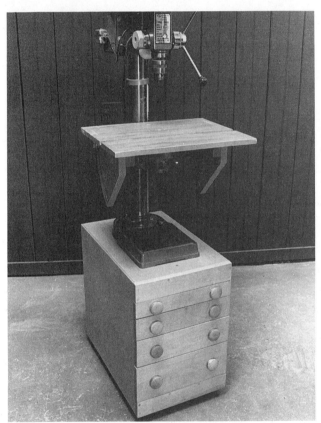

4-8 Some stationary power tools, such as this drill press, are much taller than they are wide or long. If you mount a drill press on a stand the same size as its footprint, the tool will be dangerously top-heavy. For the tool to be stable enough to use safely, the stand must be somewhat longer and wider than the drill press itself.

4-9 This band saw is used to cut a variety of materials and must be run at different speeds. To accommodate the speed changer, the stand has been made larger than it would need to be otherwise.

you may want to raise or lower a tool an inch or two from its present position. You may also want to change the level of a tool to accommodate specific types of work. *(See Figure 4-11.)* If you aren't certain whether a change in height will be a change for the better, prop your current stand up on wood blocks. Or, knock together a temporary (but sturdy) stand from construction lumber and use it at different heights for a week or two, until you find the one that works best for you. See "Space Requirements for Common Shop Tools and Fixtures" on page 10 to get an idea of the normal safe height range for specific stationary power tools.

Note: Avoid radical changes in the heights of stationary power tools. If you're used to working with a tool at a certain level and then change that level more than 2 or 3 inches, familiar operations suddenly become unfamiliar — even unsafe! Usually, a change of just an inch or two will make an enormous difference in the way a tool feels.

4-10 This radial arm saw rests on cabinets built to hold *all* the sawing accessories in the shop — not just those needed for the radial arm saw itself, but also for a circular saw, table saw, band saw, and jigsaw. Consequently the cabinets are much longer than the saw itself. The tops of the oversize cabinets also help to support long boards when you're cutting on the radial arm saw.

4-11 When you make your own tool stand, you can raise or lower the tool to accommodate the way you like to work and the type of work you do. For example, the infeed and outfeed tables of this jointer, when mounted on the factory-supplied stand, are about 32 inches from the floor — too high to be comfortable for the craftsmen who use it. So they built a new stand, lowering it about 5 inches. This also brought the top edge of the jointer fence below the work surface of the table saw. This, in turn, allows the craftsmen to keep the jointer next to the saw.

After deciding the overall dimensions of the stand, determine its configuration. To do this, consider how the tool works. The stand must not interfere with its operation or keep you from reaching the controls. For example, when designing a stand for a router table, you should leave enough room under the table for the router motor to slide up and down in its base. You must also allow access to the on/off switch, depth-of-cut adjustment, and other controls. When designing a stand for a radial arm saw, note the location of the

control that raises and lowers the arm. If it is at the front of the base, and the handle hangs down below the base, design the stand to avoid interfering with this handle. (SEE FIGURES 4-12 AND 4-13.)

Also consider how *you* work. Don't make the stand so big and bulky that you can't reach the tool comfortably. You may want to add a toe space to the stand, like that found at the bottom of kitchen cabinets. (SEE FIGURE 4-14.) A toe space allows you to stand comfortably right next to the stand without stubbing your toes.

4-12 This router table is designed to mount a plunge router. It provides easy access on all four sides so you can reach all of the switches, levers, knobs, and other controls.

4-13 On this radial arm saw, the handle that raises and lowers the arm hangs down beneath the saw base. Because of this, the front of the storage stand was built flush with the base. The cupboard doors on the stand were hung so the top door rails would be slightly below the handle.

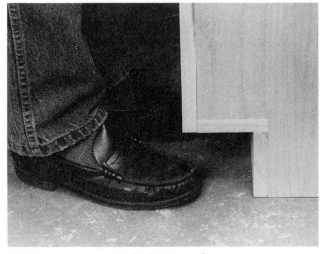

4-14 A toe space at the bottom of a tool stand provides a place to put your feet when you must stand close to the tool. These spaces are particularly important if you are to work comfortably at a stand with a footprint that is larger than the tool itself.

MOTORS, WIRING, AND DUST COLLECTION

Not all the space inside a tool stand can be used for storage if it also encloses motors, pulleys, belts, speed changers, switches, wiring, and dust collectors. Sometimes, you can mount this equipment elsewhere. For example, rather than putting a motor inside the stand, directly under the tool, you may be able to fasten it to the outside of the stand, to one side of the tool. (*SEE FIGURE 4-15.*) But other times, you will have no options. Some planers and jointers, for example, are designed so you must place the motor under the tool.

A SAFETY REMINDER

If you mount the motor on the outside of the stand, be sure to fashion a guard to protect yourself from the pulleys and belts.

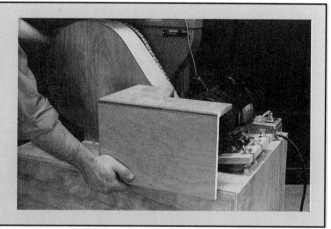

4-15 On some stationary power tools, the motor is enclosed in or attached to the tool itself. More often, however, the motor is separate and you must mount it either inside or outside the stand, as shown. If you mount it inside, you may wish to include a door in the stand to allow access to the motor, pulleys, and belt. If you fasten the motor to the outside of the stand, these things will be easily accessible; however, you must protect yourself from the moving parts by making a pulley guard.

You may have a choice of whether or not you include certain equipment in a stand. For example, dust collection is optional on many tools. On others, however, the chips must be properly evacuated for the tool to function properly, requiring you to build a dust collector into the stand. For example, on both a table saw and a jointer, the sawdust and wood chips exit from the bottom. You must cut a hole in the top of the stand for the chips to pass through, then build a dust chute, a sawdust drawer, or some other means of catching and expelling the waste from the tool. (SEE FIGURE 4-16.)

4-16 When you build a stand for a table saw, you must devise some way to evacuate the sawdust. Here are two options. On one table saw, the dust and wood chips fall into a chute. This chute funnels them into a hole in the back of the cabinet, where they are removed by a shop vacuum. The other table saw stand incorporates a sawdust drawer to catch the wood chips.

STORAGE OPTIONS

The space inside the stand that is not needed for motors, wiring, and other essential components can be used for storage. You may also use some of the vertical surfaces on the outside of the stand to hang small items. You have the same choices for storing equipment under a tool stand as you have for using the storage space under your workbench (SEE FIGURE 4-17):

■ Open shelves
■ Cupboards
■ Drawers
■ Bins
■ Pegs, hooks, and racks
■ Pegboard

The types of storage that you choose will depend on what you want to store and how often you need to use it. You might want to hang the small wrench that you use to change router bits, for example, from a peg on the front of the router table stand. However, a large routing accessory that you use less often (such as a dovetail jig) would best be stored on a shelf or in a cupboard. Likewise, if you use a set of brad-point bits constantly, arrange them in a rack on the outside of the drill press stand. Devote drawers and bins to hole saws, countersinks, plug cutters, and other drilling accessories that you use less often.

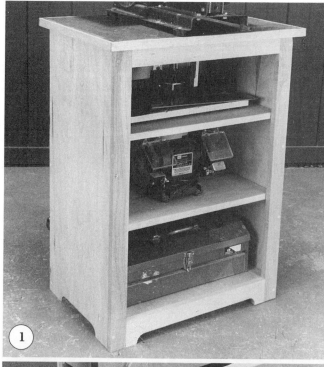

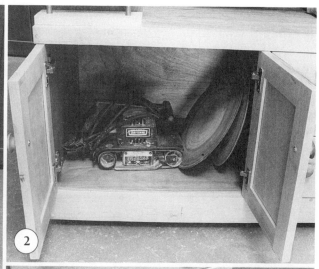

4-17 When building a tool stand, you can incorporate the same types of storage for tool accessories that you might use in a workbench. If you need the accessories to be readily accessible, you can place them on *open shelves* (1). Or, to protect these items, enclose the shelves and make *cupboards* (2). To help organize small tools and accessories, place them in *drawers* (3) or portable *bins* (4). By attaching a *rack* (5) to the tool stand, you can store accessories on the tool stand as well as in it. You can also use *pegboard* (6) to hang tools inside or outside the stand.

CUSTOMIZING YOUR TOOLS

Shop-made stands can do much more than hold tools off the ground and store related accessories. With a little imagination, you can design stands that:

- Enhance and extend the capabilities of the tool
- Combine tools
- Create original, one-of-a-kind tools

In some instances, the stand can be just as important as the tool itself! By mounting a tool creatively, you can safely extend its capacity far beyond its original limits. *FIGURES 4-18* through *4-21* show several examples of specially designed stands.

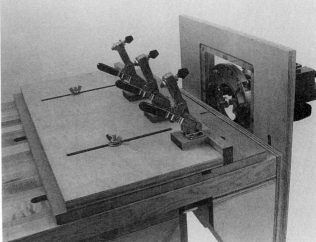

4-18 This "router workbench" appears to be an oversize routing table, but it does much more. The work surface mounts special shop-made accessories that allow you to use the router under, over, or beside the work. When the router is mounted under the work, the stand performs all the tasks of an ordinary router table. With the router suspended over the work, you can rout patterns, make signs, and cut reeds and flutes in round stock. Mounting the router horizontally beside the work makes it easy to cut mortises, tenons, and other joinery. (For details on how to build this workbench, see "Router Workbench" on page 103 of *The Workshop Companion: Advanced Routing*.)

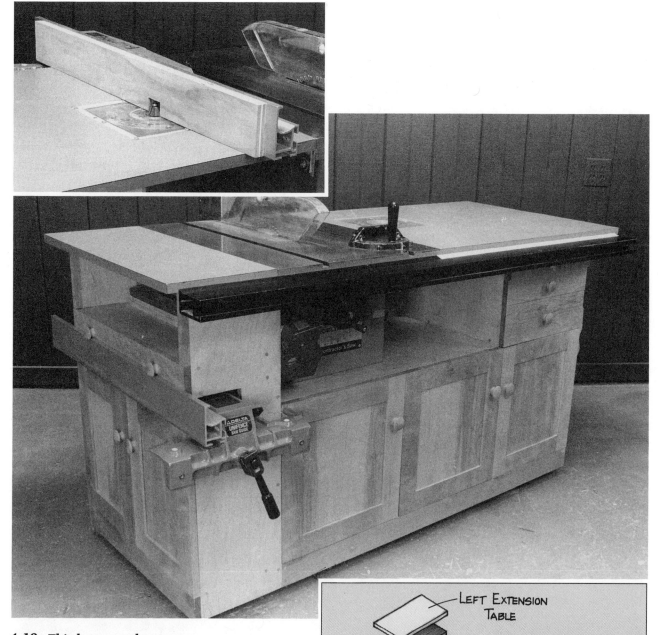

4-19 This large stand turns an ordinary contractor's table saw into a cabinet saw. It creates an enormous amount of storage under the saw, extends the right side of the work surface to increase the ripping capacity, and mounts an improved fence system. It also enables you to attach a router beneath the right table extension so the stand can do double duty as a router table. The stand looks complex to build, but it's made up of three simple plywood boxes bolted together.

4-20 This sanding station was once an old, broken-down multipurpose tool. When it sold at auction, there weren't enough pieces to make a complete working machine. So the woodworker who purchased it discarded some broken parts, modified others, and built a storage stand to mount the customized tool. Then he attached three sanding accessories — belt sander, disc sander, and drum sander. The result is a variable-speed sanding station that's more versatile than the best commercial sanders.

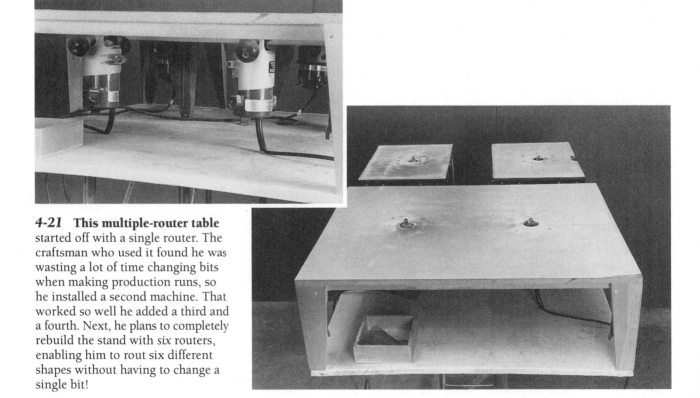

4-21 This multiple-router table started off with a single router. The craftsman who used it found he was wasting a lot of time changing bits when making production runs, so he installed a second machine. That worked so well he added a third and a fourth. Next, he plans to completely rebuild the stand with *six* routers, enabling him to rout six different shapes without having to change a single bit!

MAKING TOOLS MOBILE

You can make tools mobile simply by mounting heavy-duty casters on the bottoms of shop-made stands. Casters have several advantages. They let you move the tools in and out of storage easily — this is almost a necessity if your workshop is small or it does double duty as a garage. They also let you rearrange your tools should you want to cluster them or create more working space for a specific operation. And casters are relatively inexpensive compared to commercial accessories to make your tools mobile. You can often buy the casters and all the materials needed to make a top-notch storage stand for less than a roll-around steel frame or retractable casters.

However, casters also create several problems. For example, they may make a stand unstable. No matter how close you mount the casters to the corners of a stand, the distance between the points at which each caster contacts the floor will be *smaller* than the distance between the corners. If the distance between casters is too small, the tool will be top-heavy. To prevent this, make the footprint of the stand a little larger than you would otherwise.

Casters may also raise a stand enough to make the tool's work surface uncomfortably high. You must compensate for the height of the casters when building the stand. Remember that the nominal size given for casters isn't the overall height, but the diameter of the caster wheel. Three-inch casters, for example, are more than 3 inches tall.

Perhaps the worst problem is that tools mounted on casters often "walk" or roll across the workshop as you use them. This is not only annoying, it can be extremely dangerous: If you are passing a board across a jointer and the tool suddenly walks, your hand could slip into the knives.

To prevent accidents like this, you must have a means of locking the casters or keeping them from rolling. Effective "brake casters" (casters with dependable locking mechanisms) are, unfortunately, very expensive — four to *twenty* times the cost of ordinary swivel casters! There are, however, some inexpensive solutions. Shown here are several simple shop-made designs for making your tools mobile — and *immobile*.

1 Small and medium-size tools can be moved around like wheelbarrows. Fasten two fixed (non-swiveling) casters to one side of the stand, positioning each caster near a corner and just above the floor. You may also wish to mount handles on the opposite side of the stand. When you need to move the tool, tilt it so the feet come off the floor and the stand rests on the casters. Then roll it wherever you want it. When you put the stand down and let it come back to plumb, the casters will come off the floor and the stand will rest on its four feet.

(continued) ▷

MAKING TOOLS MOBILE — CONTINUED

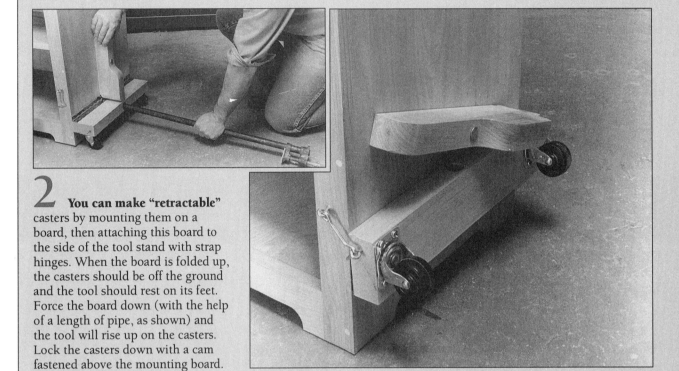

2 **You can make "retractable"** casters by mounting them on a board, then attaching this board to the side of the tool stand with strap hinges. When the board is folded up, the casters should be off the ground and the tool should rest on its feet. Force the board down (with the help of a length of pipe, as shown) and the tool will rise up on the casters. Lock the casters down with a cam fastened above the mounting board.

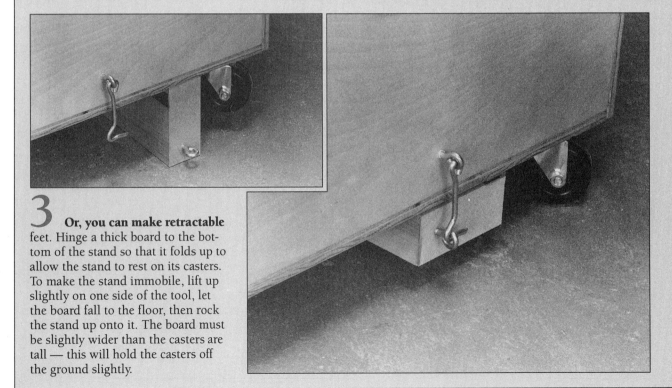

3 **Or, you can make retractable** feet. Hinge a thick board to the bottom of the stand so that it folds up to allow the stand to rest on its casters. To make the stand immobile, lift up slightly on one side of the tool, let the board fall to the floor, then rock the stand up onto it. The board must be slightly wider than the casters are tall — this will hold the casters off the ground slightly.

4 **Perhaps the simplest system** for making mobile tools immobile is to use *wedges*. These can be ordinary triangular pieces of wood that you tap into place underneath a tool stand, or they can be slightly more elaborate. Shown here are two possibilities: A *stepped wedge* lets the stand rest on a flat surface rather than the inclined edge of the wedge. This is more stable than wedges without steps. A *fitted wedge* fits around a caster to hold it from rolling or swiveling. The advantage of this device is that it doesn't need to be pounded into place.

5 **One of the most versatile** systems consists of *wedge jacks*. These devices consist of two simple wedges fastened together. To use a wedge jack, place it under a tool stand and rotate the cam lever. As you do so, one wedge will slide up the inclined plane of the other, lifting the stand off its casters. The advantage of wedge jacks is that they require no lifting or pounding to install or remove — just flip the lever. They're simple to make and can be sized to fit under almost any stand. And they can be used as leveling devices on uneven surfaces.

(continued) ▷

MAKING TOOLS MOBILE — CONTINUED

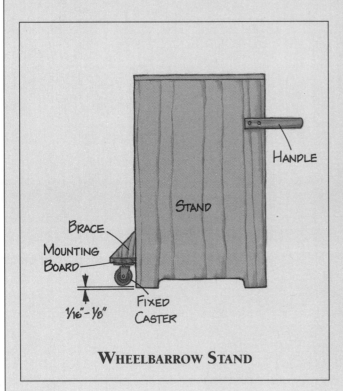

Handle

Stand

Brace
Mounting
Board
1/16" – 1/8"
Fixed
Caster

WHEELBARROW STAND

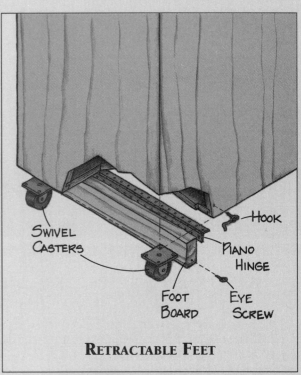

Hook

Swivel
Casters

Piano
Hinge

Foot
Board

Eye
Screw

RETRACTABLE FEET

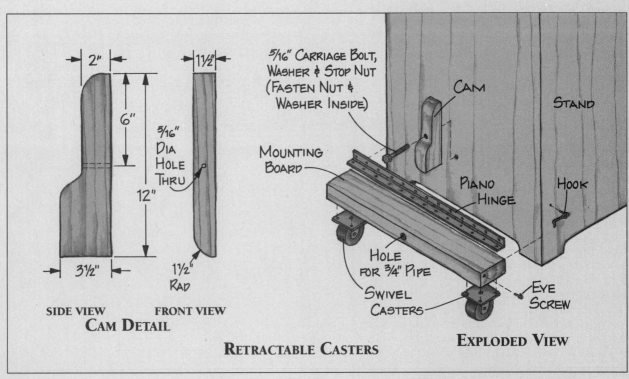

2"

1½"

6"

5/16"
Dia
Hole
Thru

12"

3½"

1½"
Rad

SIDE VIEW   FRONT VIEW

CAM DETAIL

5/16" Carriage Bolt,
Washer & Stop Nut
(Fasten Nut &
Washer Inside)

Cam

Stand

Mounting
Board

Piano
Hinge

Hook

Hole
for ¾" Pipe

Swivel
Casters

Eye
Screw

EXPLODED VIEW

RETRACTABLE CASTERS

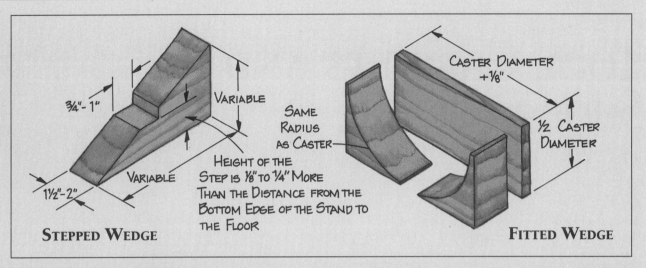

STEPPED WEDGE

3/4" - 1"

VARIABLE

VARIABLE

1 1/2" - 2"

SAME RADIUS AS CASTER

HEIGHT OF THE STEP IS 1/8" TO 1/4" MORE THAN THE DISTANCE FROM THE BOTTOM EDGE OF THE STAND TO THE FLOOR

CASTER DIAMETER + 1/8"

1/2 CASTER DIAMETER

FITTED WEDGE

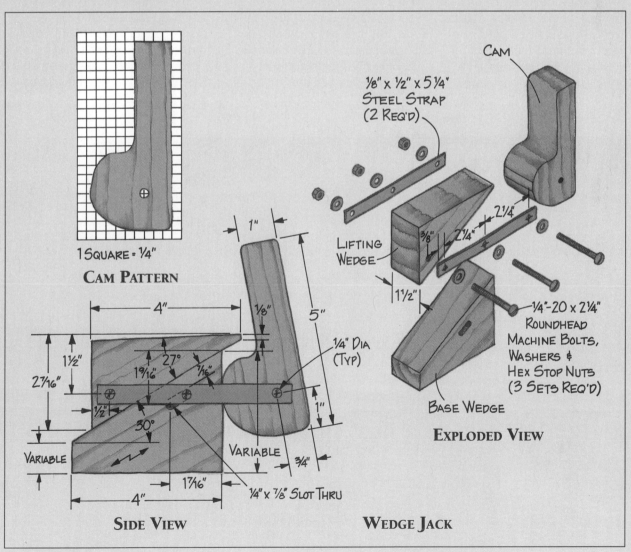

1 SQUARE = 1/4"

CAM PATTERN

CAM

1/8" x 1/2" x 5 1/4" STEEL STRAP (2 REQ'D)

LIFTING WEDGE

3/8"   2 1/4"   2 1/4"

1 1/2"

1/4"-20 x 2 1/4" ROUNDHEAD MACHINE BOLTS, WASHERS & HEX STOP NUTS (3 SETS REQ'D)

BASE WEDGE

EXPLODED VIEW

4"

1/8"

5"

1"

1/4" DIA (TYP)

1 1/2"

2 7/16"

27°

1 9/16"

7/16"

1/2"

30°

VARIABLE

1 7/16"

4"

VARIABLE

3/4"

1/4" x 7/8" SLOT THRU

SIDE VIEW

WEDGE JACK

5

TOOL CABINETS AND
SHOP STORAGE

It isn't enough to make a place to work; your workshop must also *store* your tools and materials. There must be places to hold items of every size and shape. And your storage system must allow you to locate and retrieve any one of the hundreds of items in your shop when you need it.

You can create an enormous amount of storage by building cupboards and shelves underneath workbenches and stationary power tools. But these won't satisfy all your storage needs. For example, you can't store lumber and plywood in and under your tools — you'll have to build special racks for these materials. And it often makes better sense to keep like items together, such as hardware and hand tools, so they can be easily located. Consequently, most well-organized workshops are outfitted with wood racks, pegboards, tool chests, hardware bins, and similar storage units.

TOOL CHESTS AND CABINETS

PORTABLE TOOL CHESTS AND TOTES

Woodworking was once a mobile trade. Cabinetmakers, chairmakers, finishers, and other woodworkers often traveled from town to town, looking for work. They kept their tools in a chest or cabinet that could be carried in the back of a wagon. (SEE FIGURE 5-1.)

Today, few of us could pack all our woodworking tools in the bed of a pickup, let alone in a medium-size chest. However, many craftsmen prefer to keep at least some of their tools and accessories in portable chests, bins, and trays, for several reasons.

For example, to carry often-used tools from place to place as you work, it helps to store them in a simple carryall or carpenter's tote. This is especially useful when the jobs are outside the shop. (SEE FIGURE 5-2.) If your work requires small tools, another alternative is to store them in small, transportable chests of drawers. The drawers not only help to separate and organize the tools, but often can be removed from the chests and carried to the job like small bins. (SEE FIGURE 5-3.) Some tool manufacturers sell tool chest *systems* — stacking metal chests of drawers to store small and medium-size tools. While these aren't really portable, they are *conveyable* — mounted on casters to roll around your shop. (SEE FIGURE 5-4.)

5-1 Old-time woodworkers often kept their tools in portable six-board chests, similar to this reproduction of an early-nineteenth-century tool chest that once belonged to New York cabinetmaker Duncan Phyfe. Phyfe's chest, like so many of the tool chests used by his contemporaries, was plain on the outside but elegantly worked on the inside. These woodworkers required a chest that would stand up to the rigors of travel and shop work, but they often used the workmanship inside to impress prospective clients and employers.

5-2 If you need to carry tools from one job site to another, store them in a simple carryall (*left*) or carpenter's tote (*right*). A carryall is usually smaller than a tote and doesn't have a cover or lid. A carpenter's tote is long enough to accommodate hand saws and has a lid to protect the tools from the weather. Both storage units will fit neatly on shelves in your shop when not in use.

5-3 Small, portable chests of
drawers help organize small tools
and accessories, such as screwdrivers, chisels, wrenches, drill bits,
socket sets, and so on. There are
many commercially made tool chests
available in both metal (*left*) and
wood (*right*). Or, you can make your
own — the chest in the middle was
designed and built by the craftsman
who uses it. Since the entire chest is
too large to carry easily, it splits into
two sections.

5-4 This shoulder-high metal
tool chest provides a great deal more
storage than its smaller cousins,
yet it still affords some transportabil-
ity. The chest consists of two detach-
able units. The bottom unit is a cart,
which allows you to roll the tools
around your shop. The top unit lifts
off the cart, should you need to carry
some of the tools out of the shop.

STANDING TOOL CABINETS

Not all tools need to be portable, of course, especially
if you do most of your work in your shop. Often, it
makes better sense to build a large, standing tool
cabinet to store small and medium-size tools. An ordinary cabinet, 36 inches wide, 15 inches deep, and 80
inches tall, occupies a smaller footprint than a table
saw, yet it offers over two dozen cubic feet of storage!
(In contrast, the large homemade tool chest shown in
FIGURE 5-3 provides just 1½ cubic feet.)

There are many, many possible designs for standing
cabinets. Some may be little more than a tool chest on
a stand or large plywood boxes fitted with drawers and
shelves. Others are actual pieces of fine case furniture,
adapted to hold tools and accessories. Some may be
designed to stand on the floor; others rest on a workbench. You can even adapt a piece of second-hand or
cast-off furniture as a tool cabinet. (*SEE FIGURES 5-5
THROUGH 5-7.*)

A SAFETY REMINDER

When fitting tool chests and cabinets with
drawers, think twice about using finger holes or cutouts in the drawer fronts instead of drawer pulls. Holes
and cutouts have definite advantages — they don't
protrude into your work space and there's nothing to
buy. However, if you store chisels, awls, saws, nails —
any woodworking tool or material with a point or a
cutting edge — then holes and cutouts may not be a
good idea. Since you can't see the interior of a drawer
as you stick your hand inside to open it, you could
accidently jam your finger into the business end of a
chisel or rake it along the teeth of a saw. To avoid this
problem, use drawer pulls instead.

5-5 This plywood tool cabinet is assembled with the same simple box construction described in "Tool Stands" on page 50. The lower half is fitted with drawers; the upper half is a cupboard with adjustable shelves; and the insides of the doors are covered with pegboard to hang tools.

5-6 If you prefer drawer storage, consider making a *shop highboy*. This plywood cabinet is fitted with 17 drawers, many of which are fitted with bins. Both the drawers and the bins can be easily removed and carried to wherever you're working.

5-7 This contemporary cabinet is just a case on a stand. The stand is a set of trestles, similar to the trestle frame described in "Workbenches" on page 25. The case consists of three boxes — one large box, which provides most of the storage space, and two smaller boxes, which serve as doors. The inside of the case is fitted with drawers, shelves, and racks.

SPECIALLY DESIGNED STORAGE UNITS

Some tool chests and cabinets are designed to hold just one type of tool or woodworking material. Old-time cabinetmakers often had dozens — even hundreds — of hand planes, and they sometimes built special cupboards to hold and display them. (*SEE FIGURE 5-8.*) Similarly today's woodworkers have dozens — sometimes hundreds — of clamps, and these, too, may require a special stand. (*SEE FIGURE 5-9.*) If you work with lots of finishes and solvents, you may want to invest in a fireproof cabinet. Should the volatile vapors from these chemicals accidentally ignite, this insulated metal enclosure will contain the flames and keep them from spreading. (*SEE FIGURE 5-10.*)

5-8 Craftsmen who like to work with a broad variety of planes can benefit from building special storage units for them. This cabinet was fitted with tilted shelves to make the planes easy to see and reach. The shelves are lined with felt to protect the cutting edges of the plane irons. For plans and instructions on how to make these shelves, see "Variations" on page 104.

5-9 This *clamp caddy* holds several different lengths of bar clamps, keeping them organized and easy to find. It's mounted on casters, so you can roll the clamps to wherever you're working.

5-10 This fireproof cabinet is especially designed to hold flammable liquids, such as finishes and solvents. The metal enclosure is ventilated to help keep volatile vapors from building up inside. Should the chemicals accidentally ignite, the cabinet is insulated to keep the flames from spreading.

EGG CRATES

Although drawers and bins are useful storage devices, they don't always keep their contents organized. When you stack small items in a large drawer, sooner or later they will become jumbled. And the more jumbled they become, the harder it is to find and retrieve the item you want.

The most common remedy is to make smaller drawers and bins, customizing the sizes to fit the items stored in them. This, however, can be extremely time-consuming and, for a place with as many small items as a woodworking shop, impractical. Better yet, line larger drawers and bins with an *egg crate* — a lattice of thin wooden dividers that separates the contents and keeps the items organized.

1 **To make egg crates, first** decide how thick and how deep you want the dividers to be. Don't make them too thin or they will be flimsy — ¼ inch is about as thin as you want to go. And don't make them too deep, or you will find it difficult to reach into small spaces in the assembled egg crate. Select a long, clear board from which to rip several dividers. Plane the thickness of the board to the desired width of the dividers. Cut dadoes into the face of the board, spacing them regularly every 1 to 2 inches. The width of each dado must be equal to the thickness of the finished dividers, and the depth must be exactly one-half the thickness of the board; i.e., one-half the width of the dividers.

2 **Using a table saw, rip the** dividers from the board. Keep the dadoes facing up as you cut. If they face down, there is a greater chance that the stock may chip or tear out. **Note:** You can also make these dividers from plywood. Rip the strips you need, stack them face to face, and tape the stack together.

(continued) ▷

EGG CRATES — CONTINUED

3 **Cut the dividers to length** and arrange them to run right to left and end to end in the drawers. Fit them together by lapping the dadoes. Bear in mind that the dividers don't have to be assembled in a lattice of identical square spaces. By cutting the dividers to many different lengths, you can make a lattice of different-size rectangles. Plan each rectangle to fit one of the items you will store in the drawer.

4 **Before gluing the dividers** together, line the drawer with plastic wrap or wax paper to keep the egg crate from adhering to the drawer. This will allow you to lift the grid out of the drawer when you need to clean up the sawdust. And if your storage needs change, you may want to discard this egg crate and build another.

BUILT-IN STORAGE

In addition to chests and cabinets, you can also make *built-in* storage units for your tools. Built-in cupboards, shelves, and racks aren't as versatile as stand-alone units, for the simple reason that you cannot easily rearrange them. But many of these storage devices allow you to take advantage of unused space, because they're mounted *above* the floor. And because they are attached to the shop building, they don't need to be as strong or as complex as a tool chest or cabinet. Consequently, they are not as expensive or as time-consuming to build as stand-alone furniture.

SHELVES AND RACKS

Perhaps the simplest types of built-in storage are wall-mounted shelves and racks. These turn the walls of your shop into a storage system, holding your tools and woodworking materials in plain sight.

Built-in shelves are just boards on brackets — the brackets are screwed or bolted to the wall, then the boards are mounted on the brackets. There are many commercial shelving brackets that you can buy for both fixed and adjustable shelves. You can also make your own. (SEE FIGURE 5-11.)

While shelves provide a place for tools and materials to *rest,* racks let them *hang.* Many racks are just narrow shelves with holes, slots, notches, or grooves cut in them. Others are strips of wood that mount pegs, hooks, and cleats. A Shaker peg rail is a rack of sorts, although the pegs in a traditional rail are too far apart to make the best use of the wall space in a modern workshop. You can improve on this old design by using smaller pegs and spacing them closer together. Or, cover an entire section of a wall with pegs. (*SEE FIGURE 5-12.*)

TRY THIS TRICK

To make the best use of your wall space, you might combine shelves and racks. For example, cut notches in the front edge of a shelf to hang small tools, or mount a shelf over a peg rail to create both resting and hanging storage.

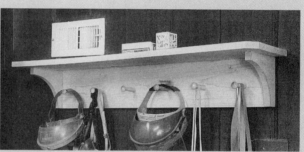

5-11 To mount small and medium-size shelves (up to 12 inches wide) on a wall, attach the supports to the studs in the wall frame. You can purchase many different commercially made shelving supports. With metal standards and brackets, for example, you can create an *adjustable* built-in shelving system (1). Or, you can make your own brackets from scraps of wood and plywood (2). If you need to mount a wide shelf or one that must support a great deal of weight, use chains or cables to keep the outer edge from drooping (3).

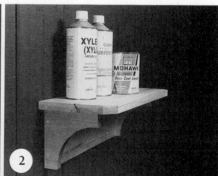

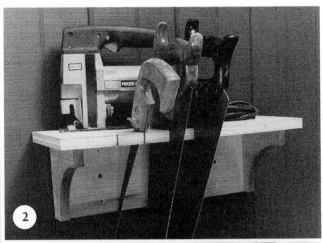

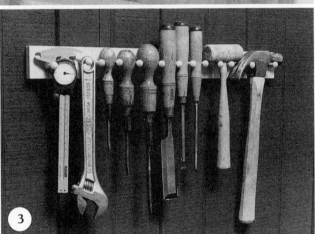

5-12 One of the simplest racks is a narrow shelf with holes, notches, slots, and grooves cut in it (1 and 2). You can also mount a row of pegs in a strip of wood, similar to an old Shaker peg rail (3). If a single row of pegs won't do, screw a board to the wall and cover it with pegs (4). Or, use any combination of these hangers.

Perhaps the most versatile and widely used hanging storage systems are commercial pegboards. A sheet of pegboard converts the wall space that it covers to a huge, adjustable rack. There are many different types of metal hangers available for pegboard, and these can be mounted anywhere on a pegboard-covered wall. You can easily switch or rearrange these hangers as your storage needs change. (SEE FIGURE 5-13.)

If ordinary, generic hanging storage devices won't do, you can design special racks to hold specific tools. This requires a little creativity. You must decide what part of the tool needs to be held, then build a hanger to fit it. (SEE FIGURE 5-14.)

5-13 Commercial pegboard holds many types of metal hangers. When mounted on a wall, the entire board becomes an adjustable rack. Because of the way in which the hangers are inserted in the pegboard holes, the pegboard must be mounted about ½ inch *away* from the wall, as shown. Nail up strips of wood to the wall studs to serve as spacers, then attach the pegboard to those strips.

5-14 If you aren't satisfied with ordinary pegs and hooks, you can make specially fitted racks for specific tools. This special rack, designed by Debbie Van Bokern of Cincinnati, Ohio, holds measuring tools.

BUILT-IN CUPBOARDS AND COUNTERS

If you prefer not to store your woodworking tools on open shelves and racks, enclose them in cupboards. Hanging cupboards protect their contents from dust; they can be locked to prevent children and unauthorized persons from messing with your stuff; and they reduce the visual clutter, making your shop a more pleasant place to spend time. (*SEE FIGURE 5-15.*)

Or, store your tools in counter units — these cupboards are still attached to the wall, but they rest on the floor like built-in kitchen counters with workbench tops. These counters not only store and protect the tools, but also provide extra work space. (*SEE FIGURE 5-16.*)

Although they are built from less expensive materials, both the hanging cupboards and the counters are built in a manner similar to the cabinet systems

that you might install in a kitchen or bathroom. They are also installed in much the same way. It is best to build them as independent units, small enough to be easily manageable. The counters are installed by scooting them into place, leveling them with wedges, then bolting the backs to the studs in the wall. The cupboards must be held up against the walls with braces (or strong helpers), leveled, then bolted in place.

Both the hanging cupboards and the counters are attached to the shop wall and can't be easily moved about; however, it's not impossible to move them. Should you need to rearrange your shop — or should you move your shop and want to take all the storage units with you — you can detach them from the wall simply by removing the lag screws that hold them to the studs.

5-15 This hanging cupboard
encloses both shelves and racks. It's
secured to the wall with lag screws.
The screws are driven through a cleat
in the back top corner of the cupboard
and into the studs in the wall.

5-16 This counter unit has a
benchtop made of particleboard
covered with hardboard. The unit
provides work space as well as storage
space. Like the hanging cupboards,
it's attached to the studs in the wall
by cleats in the back of the unit.

WOOD STORAGE

Second only to your stationary power tools, the item
that takes up the most room in your workshop is the
stuff you work with — wood and plywood. You may
be able to store the bulk of your lumber outside your
shop, in a barn, storage shed, or garage. However, it's
extremely important to have at least *some* wood storage
in your shop. This allows the wood to become accli-
mated to the shop environment, so its moisture con-
tent reaches an equilibrium with the indoor relative
humidity *before* you work on it. If you don't have the
means to "shop-dry" the wood for a few weeks before
working with it, the boards may expand or contract
noticeably *after* you cut them to size. This, in turn,
will affect the fit of the joints.

Wood is usually stored in racks, either horizontal
or vertical. It's okay to store wood vertically for short
periods of time. But horizontally is preferred, especially
for long boards stored more than a few weeks —
otherwise, they may flex and bow.

FOR BEST RESULTS

If you need absolutely straight wood for door
frames or drawer sides, don't let the boards shop-dry
vertically. Store them horizontally from the moment
you bring them into the shop.

A vertical rack can be as simple as a spot on a wall
to lean the boards against. Or, you can make peg rails
or large bins to help organize the lumber. (*SEE FIGURE
5-17.*)

Although horizontal racks require more space than
vertical ones, they can be built overhead in otherwise
unused space if the ceilings in your shop are sufficiently high. However, most horizontal racks hold
lumber on rails that are supported either on both ends
(called *closed racks*) or on just one end (*open racks*).

To use a closed rack, you must stack the wood and remove it from the *ends* — this can be difficult and time-consuming, particularly when you need to retrieve a long board from the middle of a stack. (*SEE FIGURE 5-18.*) When using an open rack, you can access the wood on the rack from the *side* and save yourself considerable aggravation. (*SEE FIGURE 5-19.*) However, it's much easier to build a closed wood rack than an open one. The rails on open racks must be stronger and require more bracework.

In addition to storage racks for long boards, you also need a convenient way to gather the "shorts" — scraps that are too valuable to throw away. They can be held vertically in a simple bin, allowing you to rummage through the boards and retrieve the ones you want, like files from a filing cabinet. (*SEE FIGURE 5-20.*) There is little danger that shorts will bow when stored vertically, since they flex much less than long boards and are already shop-dried.

5-17 If your shop has a high ceiling but limited floor space, consider making a vertical wood rack to hold long boards on end. It's mounted on casters, so you can roll the wood around the shop if you need to.

5-18 This closed rack consists of vertical two-by-fours with holes drilled in them to hold short lengths of 1¼-inch-diameter closet pole. These pieces of closet pole serve as the rails that support the lumber. Each rail is adjustable — you can change its height by moving it to another set of holes in the supports. To stack lumber in the rack, you slide the boards in from the ends.

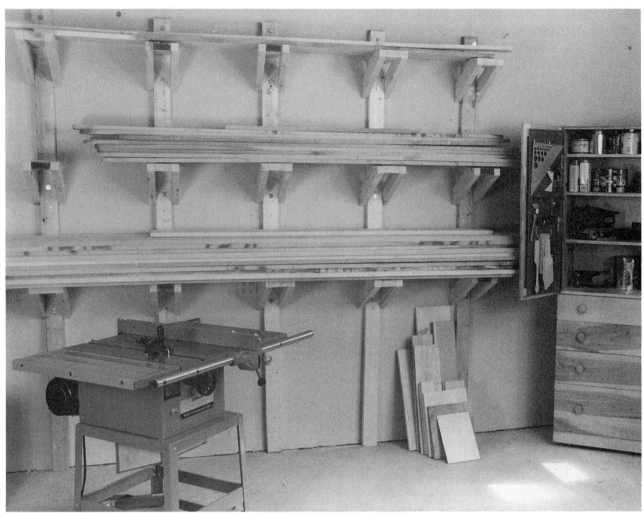

5-19 This open rack is made
entirely from two-by-four stock. The
supports are bolted to the studs in
the wall, then the braces are screwed
to the supports. The brackets aren't
adjustable; you cannot change their
height. However, it's much easier to
stack wood on this rack than on a
closed one — you simply lift each
board onto the brackets from the
side.

5-20 **This rolling bin provides**
storage for "shorts" — usable wood
scraps. The boards are placed in the
bin vertically, allowing you to flip
through them easily. Some craftsmen
install dividers in their shorts bins to
help keep the wood organized. But
this design limits the width of the
boards you can install between each
set of dividers, and the woodworker
who made this divider-less bin preferred to organize his short boards by
the type of wood rather than width.

ATTACHING SHELVES AND CABINETS TO WALLS

Built-in storage systems aren't really built in. Instead, they are assembled as units, much as you'd assemble a piece of stand-alone shop furniture. Then they are attached to the wall of your workshop.

How you attach them depends on how the wall is built. There are two common types of walls — frame and masonry.

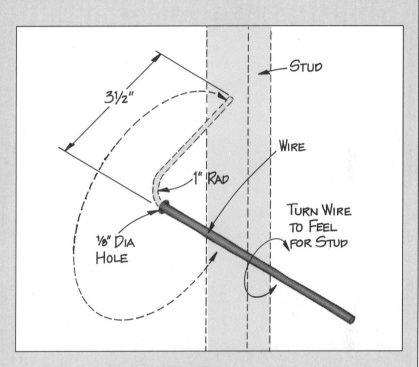

1 **If you have a frame wall, you** want to attach the storage units to the vertical two-by-four *studs* in that wall. To find them, tap along the wall with a hammer. When the tapping sounds more solid and the pitch rises, you're over a stud. Drill several small holes through the plaster or drywall to find the exact location. If you still have trouble locating the stud, feel for it with an L-shaped length of coat hanger, as shown.

2 **When you know the exact** locations of the studs, tap a nail into the wall near the top of each stud and another near the bottom. Snap a line between the two nails to mark the stud location on the wall, then remove the nails. If the built-ins won't cover all the holes you created by drilling and pounding nails, patch the holes with spackling.

(continued) ▷

ATTACHING SHELVES AND CABINETS TO WALLS — CONTINUED

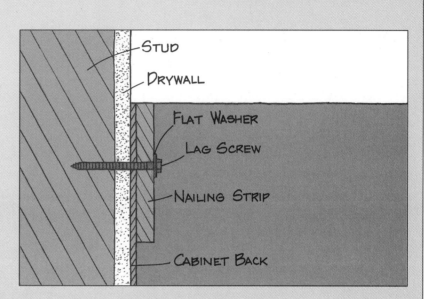

3 **Place the shelf or cabinet** against the wall. If you are hanging it, brace it at the proper height. If the unit is light enough, have a helper hold it for a moment. If it's fairly heavy, build a simple scaffold from construction lumber to rest it on. Level the unit, then drive lag screws through the back of the unit and into the studs.

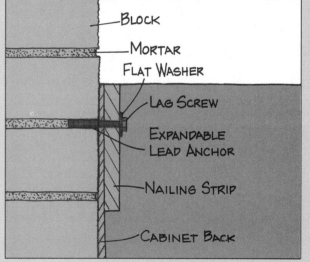

4 **If you have a masonry wall,** you have considerably more latitude on where you can attach your built-ins. However, you must first drill holes and install *lead anchors* in the masonry to hold the screws. If the wall is made from concrete block or brick, drill holes in the mortar between them, using a drill and a masonry bit. If the wall is made of concrete, you can poke a hole anywhere, but it will take a lot of time.

5 **Place expandable lead** anchors in the holes you have drilled. Position the storage units and level them, then drive lag screws through the shelving brackets or cabinet backs and into the anchors.

PROJECTS

6

STORAGE STAND

This wooden tool stand design offers several benefits. First — and most important — it's sturdy. The box construction is, in fact, stronger and more stable than most commercial metal stands that are sold with stationary power tools. It's versatile — you can adjust the dimensions and the configuration to support almost any large power tool. It can even be made into a bench to store and support bench-top tools. And it's inexpensive — the stand shown was made from ordinary utility wood and shop-grade plywood.

The interior of the stand is mostly hollow and will accommodate motors, wiring, and dust collection equipment. Any leftover space inside the stand can be used to store tool accessories, jigs, and materials. As shown, the stand has a cupboard with adjustable shelves on one side and drawers on the other. However, it can easily be reconfigured with a different combination of storage devices, depending on your needs.

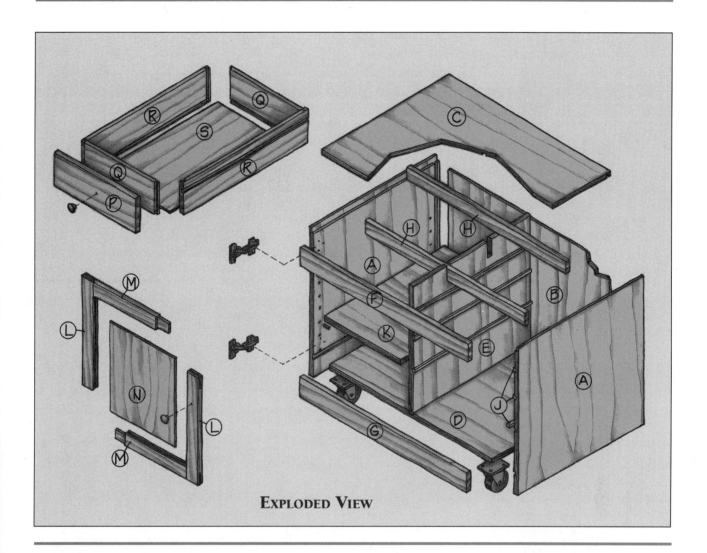

EXPLODED VIEW

MATERIALS LIST (FINISHED DIMENSIONS)

Parts

A. Sides* (2) — ¾" x (variable) x (variable)

B. Back* — ¾" x (variable) x (variable)

C. Top* — ¾" x (variable) x (variable)

D. Bottom* — ¾" x (variable) x (variable)

E. Divider* — ¾" x (variable) x (variable)

F. Top rail — ¾" x 2¾" x (variable)

G. Bottom rail — ¾" x 3⅛" x (variable)

H. Braces (2†) — ¾" x 2" x (variable)

J. Drawer guides (6) — ½" x ½" x (variable)

K. Adjustable shelves* — ¾" x (variable) x (variable)

L. Door stiles (2) — ¾" x 2" x (variable)

M. Door rails (2) — ¾" x 2" x (variable)

N. Door panel* — ¼" x (variable) x (variable)

P. Drawer faces (3) — ¾" x (variable) x (variable)

Q. Drawer fronts/ backs (6) — ½" x (variable) x (variable)

R. Drawer sides (6) — ½" x (variable) x (variable)

S. Drawer bottoms* (3) — ¼" x (variable) x (variable)

*Make these parts from plywood.
†If the tool is large or extremely heavy, add more braces.

Hardware

#8 x 1¼" Flathead wood screws (36–48)

¼" Shelving support pins (4)

1½" Drawer pulls (4)

European-style self-closing cabinet hinges for overlay doors and mounting screws (2)

3" Heavy-duty swivel casters and mounting screws (4)

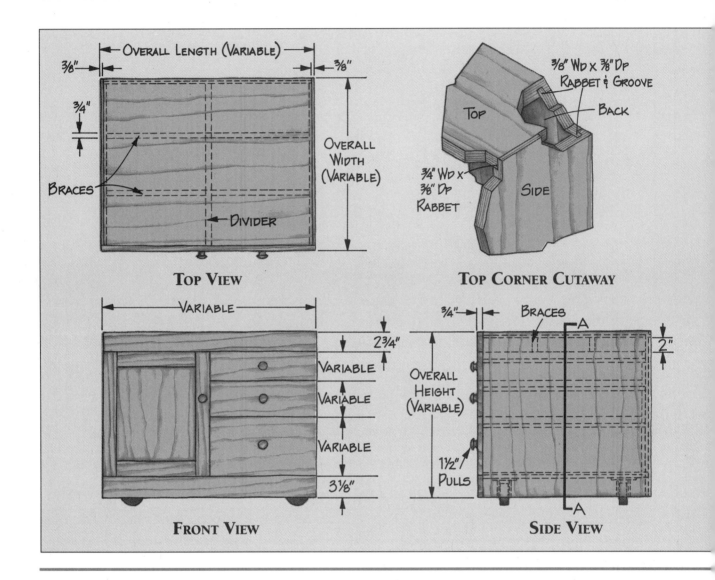

TOP VIEW

TOP CORNER CUTAWAY

FRONT VIEW

SIDE VIEW

PLAN OF PROCEDURE

1 Adapt the plans to fit your requirements.
The storage stand must be sized to fit the tool you want it to support, and configured to provide the storage you need. Because of this, many of the dimensions in the Materials List and on the working drawings are labeled "variable" — fill in these missing measurements before beginning construction.

First consider the overall size of the stand. How long and how wide must the stand be to provide a stable base for the tool? How high should it be to hold the tool's work surface at a comfortable height?

Next, consider its configuration. As shown, the stand is divided into two halves, with drawers in one half and cupboard space in the other. You may wish to convert both halves into cupboard space or fit both halves with drawers. You may wish to add more dividers or eliminate them altogether. The configuration will depend on the size of the stand, the location of the motor and other essential equipment, and what you wish to store in the stand.

You can also change the construction details, if necessary. For example, if you want lots of shallow drawers to store small items, you can stack more than three drawers on top of one another. If you want to hang tools on the door, mount pegboard on the inside surface and use piano hinges to support the additional weight. If you don't need the tool to be mobile, eliminate the casters and cut the bottom edges of the stand to create feet. (*SEE FIGURE 6-1.*) For more options, see "Designing a Storage Stand" on page 50.

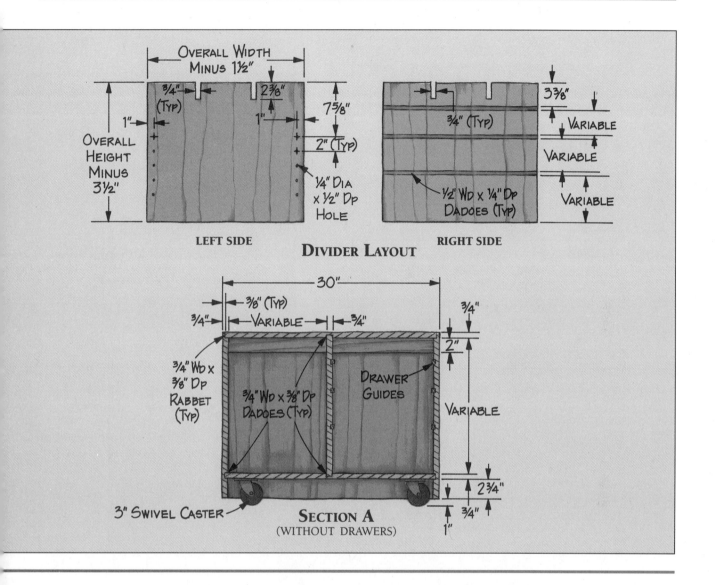

OVERALL WIDTH
MINUS 1½"

¾"
(TYP)

2⅜"

1"

1"

7⅝"

2" (TYP)

¼" DIA
x ½" DP
HOLE

OVERALL
HEIGHT
MINUS
3½"

LEFT SIDE

3⅜"

¾" (TYP)

VARIABLE

VARIABLE

VARIABLE

½" WD x ¼" DP
DADOES (TYP)

RIGHT SIDE

DIVIDER LAYOUT

30"

⅜" (TYP)

¾"

VARIABLE

¾"

¾" WD x
⅜" DP
RABBET
(TYP)

¾" WD x ⅜" DP
DADOES (TYP)

DRAWER
GUIDES

¾"

2"

VARIABLE

2¾"

3" SWIVEL CASTER

SECTION A
(WITHOUT DRAWERS)

¾"

1"

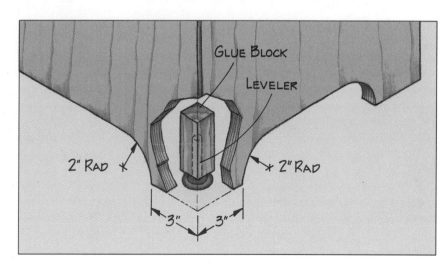

6-1 If you don't mount the stand
on casters, relieve the bottom edges
of sides, back, and bottom rail to
create feet. Separate feet will rest
more steadily on a shop floor that
isn't perfectly level. If the floor is
visibly uneven, install a glue block
and a furniture leveler behind each
foot. This will let you extend the feet
slightly to compensate for the uneven surface.

GLUE BLOCK

LEVELER

2" RAD

2" RAD

3"

3"

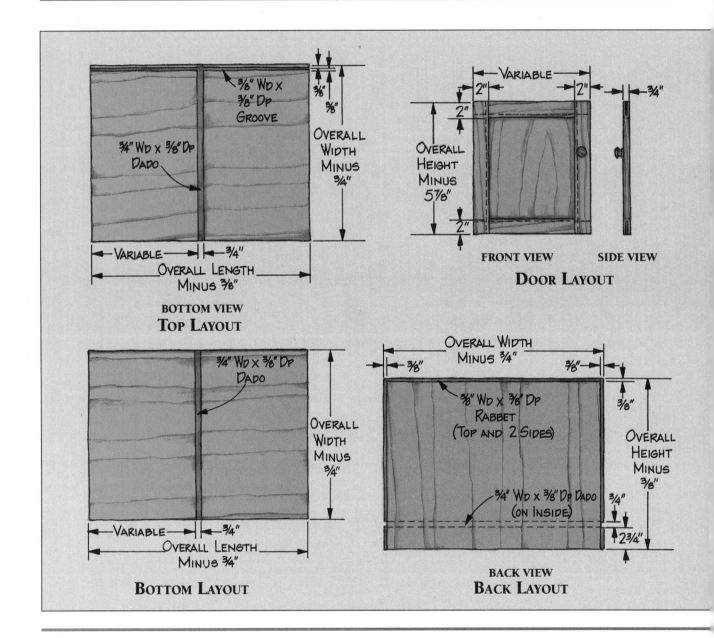

BOTTOM VIEW
TOP LAYOUT

DOOR LAYOUT

BOTTOM LAYOUT

BACK VIEW
BACK LAYOUT

2 Cut the case parts to size. Once you know the overall size of the stand and the arrangement of doors and drawers, determine the number of parts and their dimensions. *Double-check your figures* — although this is a simple project, there are a lot of measurements to calculate.

Figure the amounts of wood and plywood that you need, and purchase the materials. The stand shown is made from solid maple and birch plywood — attractive but relatively inexpensive materials. Depending on your tastes and your budget, you can use almost any reasonably straight, clear wood and shop-grade plywood.

Cut the parts for the case — sides, back, top, bottom, divider, braces, and drawer guides. Also cut the adjustable shelves, but do *not* cut the door or drawer parts yet. Wait until after you have assembled the case.

3 Cut the joinery in the case parts. To make the stand as sturdy as possible, the major structural parts are all assembled with interlocking rabbets, dadoes, grooves, and notches. Cut these joints with a router or a dado cutter:

■ ³⁄₄-inch-wide, ³⁄₈-inch-deep rabbets in the top edges of the sides to hold the top, as shown in the *Left Side Layout* and *Right Side Layout*

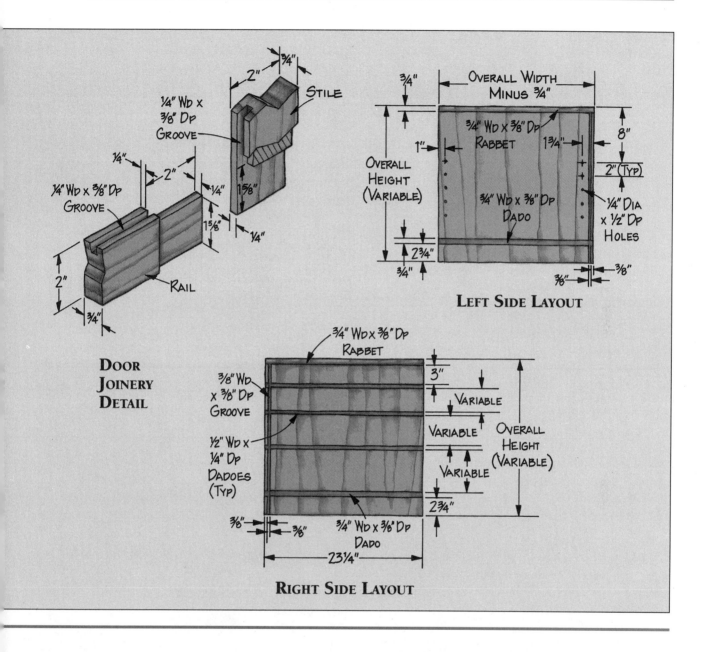

DOOR JOINERY DETAIL

LEFT SIDE LAYOUT

RIGHT SIDE LAYOUT

■ ³/₄-inch-wide, ³/₈-inch-deep dadoes near the bottom edges of the sides and back to hold the bottom, as shown in the *Left Side Layout, Right Side Layout,* and *Back Layout*

■ ³/₄-inch-wide, ³/₈-inch-deep dadoes in the top and the bottom to hold the divider, as shown in the *Top Layout* and *Bottom Layout*

■ ³/₈-inch-wide, ³/₈-inch-deep grooves near the back edges of the sides to hold the back, as shown in the *Left Side Layout* and *Right Side Layout*

■ one ³/₈-inch-wide, ³/₈-inch-deep groove near the back edge of the top to hold the back, as shown in the *Top Layout*

■ ³/₈-inch-wide, ³/₈-inch-deep rabbets in the top and side edges of the back to fit the grooves in the top and sides, as shown in the *Back Layout*

If you are mounting drawers in the stand, rout ¹/₂-inch-wide, ¹/₄-inch-deep dadoes in the sides and dividers, as shown in the *Right Side Layout* and *Divider Layout/Right Side.* **Note:** The top edge of the divider is ³/₈ inch lower than the top edge of the side so the dadoes are ³/₈ inch closer to the edge, as shown.

Using a saber saw or a coping saw, cut ³/₄-inch-wide, 2³/₈-inch-deep notches in the divider, as shown in the *Divider Layout/Left Side.* These notches fit around the braces.

4   Drill holes in the sides and dividers for shelf supports. If you have elected to mount adjustable shelves in the stand, drill 1/4-inch-diameter, 1/2-inch-deep holes in the appropriate sides and dividers, as shown in the *Left Side Layout* and *Divider Layout/Left Side*. These holes will hold shelving support pins. **Note:** The holes in the divider are not in the same vertical location as those in the side. This, too, is because the divider is slightly below the side in the assembled case.

5   Assemble the case. Dry assemble (with*out* glue) the parts of the case to test the fit of the joints. When you're satisfied the joints fit properly, disassemble the case and lightly sand the inside surfaces of the parts.

Glue the drawer guides in the sides and dividers. When the glue is dry, assemble the sides, back, and bottom with glue and #8 screws. Drive the screws from the outside, countersinking and counterboring each screw so the head rests about 1/16 inch below the plywood surface.

Glue the divider to the bottom and the back. Drive screws up through the bottom and into the divider. However, don't screw the back to the divider yet. Glue the braces and the top to the assembly; check that the case is square; then screw together all the glue joints that haven't yet been reinforced with screws. Once again, countersink and counterbore the screws.

Attach the top and bottom rails to the assembly with glue and screws. Note that the top edge of the bottom rail is 3/8 inch below the top surface of the bottom. This lets you use the front edge of the bottom as a stop for the door and drawers.

Cover all the screw heads that show on the outside of the case with wood plugs. Let the glue dry; then sand the plugs flush with the plywood surface. Also sand the outside corners clean and flush.

Note: Because this stand will be used in your workshop, the design makes no attempt to hide all the edges of the plywood. There will be plies visible at several corners. If you wish to cover these, rout shallow rabbets at the corners of the assembled case and glue strips of matching veneer over the plies.

6   Cut the parts for the door and drawers. Measure the openings for the door and drawers in the assembled case. If the measurements differ from what you expected, adjust the dimensions of the door and drawers accordingly. Figure the sizes of the door and drawer parts, then cut them.

The doors and drawers must be slightly smaller than their openings to work properly. However, *don't* cut the parts small. Instead, make them so the assembled doors and drawers will be the same size as the openings, then sand or plane the assemblies to fit. Also remember that the door frame and drawer faces overlap the front edges of the sides completely, but they only overlap the divider half way.

7   Cut the door joinery. The door panel rests in a groove in the frame parts, and the frame is assembled with simple bridle joints, as shown in the *Door Joinery Detail*. You can make both of these joints with a router or a dado cutter.

First, cut 1/4-inch-wide, 3/8-inch-deep grooves in the *inside* edges of the door rails and stiles. Next, cut a 1/4-inch-wide, 15/8-inch-deep notch in each end of each stile. Finally, cut two 2-inch-wide, 1/4-inch-deep rabbets in each end of each rail. Each pair of rabbets will form a 1/4-inch-thick, 2-inch-long tenon to fit the notch in the adjoining stile.

6-2   For easy installation, a European-style cabinet hinge comes apart in two pieces — the hinge itself and its mounting plate. The hinge part is attached to the door frame stile, and its plate to the inside of the case. To mount the hinge part, drill a 13/8-inch-diameter, 1/2-inch-deep hole in the stile. Place the hinge housing in the hole and secure it with screws.

8 Assemble and hang the door. Lightly sand the door parts. Glue the door rails and stiles together. As you do so, slip the panel into its grooves. However, do *not* glue the panel in place. Let it "float" in the grooves.

Sand or plane the assembled door frame to fit the case, then mark the locations of the hinges on the door and the inside of the case. To mount European-style cabinet hinges, drill 1³/₈-inch-diameter (or 35-millimeter-diameter), ¹/₂-inch-deep holes in the door stile, and drill pilot holes for the mounting screws inside the case. Insert the round housing for each hinge in the large hole in the door frame, then screw the mounting plate to the case. Adjust the hinges to position the door on the case, then mount a pull on the door. (*SEE FIGURES 6-2 THROUGH 6-4.*)

9 Cut the drawer joinery. The front and back of each drawer is joined to the sides with rabbets and dadoes. The bottom rests in grooves inside the front, back, and sides; and the drawer face is simply glued to the front. The drawers slide in and out of the case on the drawer guides, and these guides fit into grooves in the drawer sides.

Using a router or a dado cutter, cut ¹/₄-inch-wide, ¹/₄-inch-deep grooves in the inside faces of the front, back, and sides, near the bottom edge, as shown in the *Drawer/Side View.* Also cut ¹/₄-inch-wide, ¹/₄-inch-deep dadoes near the ends of the sides, and ¹/₄-inch-wide, ¹/₄-inch-deep rabbets in the ends of the fronts and backs. Finally, cut ¹⁷/₃₂-inch-wide, ⁹/₃₂-inch-deep grooves in the *outside* faces of the drawer sides for the drawer guides.

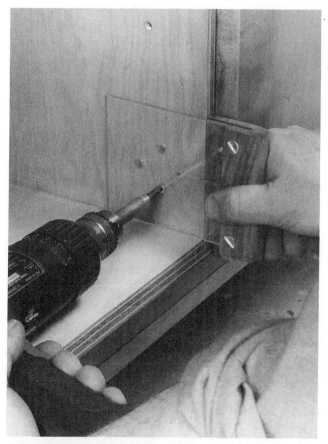

6-3 Drill ¹/₈-inch-diameter pilot holes inside the case for the mounting plate screws. There are commercial templates (shown) available to help you locate these holes; you also can use the mounting plates themselves to mark the screw positions. Attach the mounting plate to the case.

6-4 Extend the hinge arm, slip it over the mounting plate, and tighten the locking screw that holds the parts together. Close the door to see how it fits. If necessary, use the adjusting screws on the hinge to move the door slightly in or out, up or down, right or left, until it fits properly.

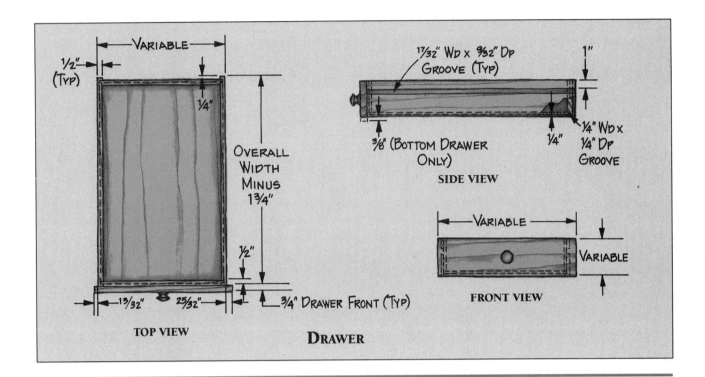

DRAWER

TOP VIEW

SIDE VIEW

FRONT VIEW

10 Assemble and install the drawers. Lightly sand the drawer parts. Glue the drawer fronts, backs, and sides together. As you do so, slide the bottoms into their grooves. However, do *not* glue the bottoms in place. Like the door panel, they should be allowed to float in their grooves. Also, do *not* glue the drawer faces to the fronts yet.

Slide the drawers into the case, fitting the grooves to the drawer guides. If any of the drawers bind in the case, sand or plane the sides until they slide in and out easily. Then remove the drawers.

Lay the case on its back and place scraps of ¼-inch plywood on the inside surface of the back to serve as spacers. Slide the drawers all the way into the case — the spacers should hold the drawer fronts flush with the front edges of the case. Place the drawer faces over the fronts, fitting them so there's a ¹⁄₃₂- to ¹⁄₁₆-inch gap between the faces and the adjoining door frame. Temporarily tape or clamp the faces to the case; then drill ⅛-inch-diameter pilot holes through the faces *and* the fronts where you will later attach drawer pulls.

Remove the drawer faces, spread glue on the drawer fronts, and lay the faces back in place. Clamp the faces to the fronts by temporarily driving #8 screws through the pilot holes in the faces and into the fronts. Remove the drawers from the case and apply hand screws. When the glue sets up, back the screws out of the pilot holes. Enlarge the holes and mount drawer pulls.

11 Finish the stand. Remove the doors and drawers from the case, and remove the hinge parts from the door and case. Do any necessary finish sanding on the case, adjustable shelves, door, and drawers. Then apply several coats of tung oil to all wood surfaces, letting the oil dry thoroughly between each coat. Rub out the last coat with #0000 steel wool and paste wax — the wax will help the finish resist glue spills and other abuse. Also wax the drawer guides to help the drawers slide smoothly.

12 Mount the tool on the stand. Turn the stand on its top and attach the casters to the bottom. Mount the casters as close to the corners as possible, but not so close that the wheels bump into the case parts when they swivel.

Turn the stand right side up and attach the tool to the top with carriage bolts. If necessary, mount the dust collection equipment and the motor inside the stand. Also install a switch in a convenient location, an electrical cord, and any other necessary wiring.

When the tool is running properly, replace the door and drawers. If you have elected to mount adjustable shelves inside the stand, insert metal shelving support pins in the appropriate holes, then rest the shelves on the pins.

7

HAND TOOL CABINET

If you like to work wood by hand, you'll appreciate this cabinet. It's designed to store and organize all kinds and sizes of hand tools. Most craftsmen still rely on hand tools in their woodworking — you can't do everything on a machine, and some woodworking tasks go faster and better by hand than with power tools. As shown, this cabinet is configured for planes, scrapers, and chisels. But it will also hold layout tools, hand saws, mallets, screwdrivers — almost any small or medium-size woodworking tool. You can hang tools inside the doors on adjustable racks, rest them on adjustable shelves, or place them in drawers.

This cabinet not only stores tools, but also helps protect them from rust. Hand tools often rust during humid weather, but if you bathe them in the vapors of evaporating *camphor,* a thin, rust-preventing coat will form on the surface of the metal. Holes in the drawer bottoms and fixed shelves allow the camphor vapors to circulate freely inside the cabinet. Place a small amount of camphor (available as blocks or crystals from most drugstores) in the bottom drawers, and the vapors will reach *all* the tools in the cabinet.

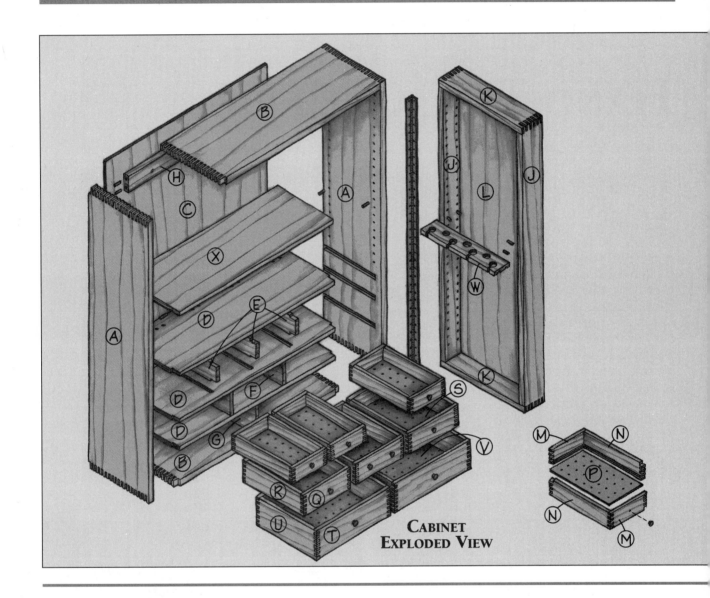

**CABINET
EXPLODED VIEW**

MATERIALS LIST (FINISHED DIMENSIONS)

Parts

Cabinet

A. Case sides (2) $\frac{3}{4}'' \times 9'' \times 36''$

B. Case top/
   bottom (2) $\frac{3}{4}'' \times 9'' \times 25''$

C. Back panel* $\frac{1}{4}'' \times 24'' \times 35''$

D. Fixed
   shelves (3) $\frac{1}{2}'' \times 8\frac{3}{4}'' \times 24''$

E. Upper drawer
   dividers (3) $\frac{1}{2}'' \times 8\frac{3}{4}'' \times 2\frac{1}{2}''$

F. Middle drawer
   dividers (2) $\frac{1}{2}'' \times 8\frac{3}{4}'' \times 3\frac{1}{2}''$

G. Lower drawer
   divider $\frac{1}{2}'' \times 8\frac{3}{4}'' \times 4\frac{1}{2}''$

H. Hanger $\frac{3}{4}'' \times 2'' \times 23\frac{1}{2}''$

J. Door sides (4) $\frac{3}{4}'' \times 3'' \times 36''$

K. Door tops/
   bottoms (4) $\frac{3}{4}'' \times 3'' \times 12\frac{1}{2}''$

L. Door panels
   (2) $\frac{1}{2}'' \times 11\frac{5}{8}'' \times 35\frac{3}{16}''$

M. Upper drawer fronts/
   backs (8) $\frac{3}{8}'' \times 2'' \times 5\frac{1}{2}''$

N. Upper drawer
   sides (8) $\frac{3}{8}'' \times 2'' \times 8\frac{3}{4}''$

P. Upper drawer
   bottoms† (4) $\frac{1}{8}'' \times 5\frac{1}{8}'' \times 8\frac{3}{8}''$

Q. Middle drawer fronts/
   backs (6) $\frac{3}{8}'' \times 3'' \times 7\frac{1}{2}''$

R. Middle drawer
   sides (6) $\frac{3}{8}'' \times 3'' \times 8\frac{3}{4}''$

S. Middle drawer
   bottoms† (3) $\frac{1}{8}'' \times 7\frac{1}{8}'' \times 8\frac{3}{8}''$

T. Lower drawer fronts/
   backs (4) $\frac{3}{8}'' \times 4'' \times 11\frac{1}{2}''$

U. Lower drawer
   sides (4) $\frac{3}{8}'' \times 4'' \times 8\frac{3}{4}''$

V. Lower drawer bottoms†
   (2) $\frac{1}{8}'' \times 11\frac{1}{8}'' \times 8\frac{3}{8}''$

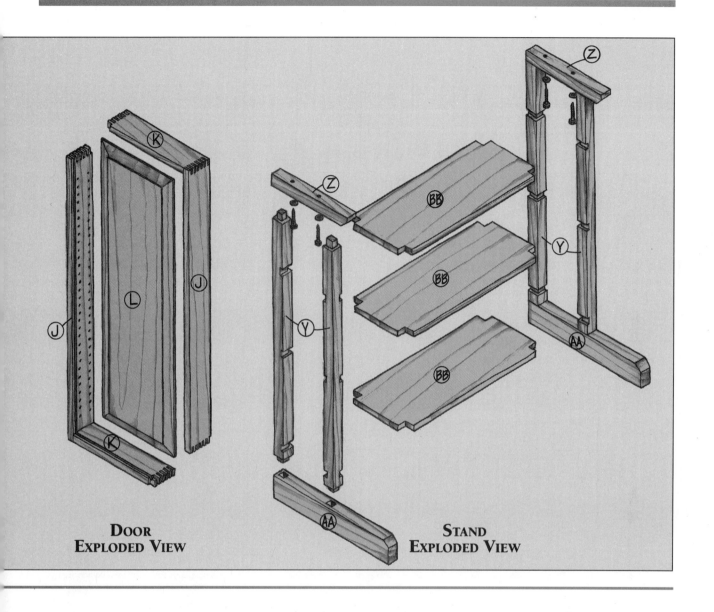

**DOOR
EXPLODED VIEW**

**STAND
EXPLODED VIEW**

Hardware

W. Adjustable racks (2–6) $\frac{1}{2}$" x $2\frac{1}{2}$" x $10^{15}/_{16}$"

X. Adjustable shelves (1–3) $\frac{1}{2}$" x $8\frac{3}{4}$" x $23^{7}/_{16}$"

Stand (optional)

Y. Legs (4) $1\frac{1}{2}$" x $1\frac{1}{2}$" x $33\frac{1}{2}$"
Z. Braces (2) $1\frac{1}{2}$" x $1\frac{1}{2}$" x 12"
AA. Feet (2) $1\frac{1}{2}$" x 3" x 18"
BB. Stand shelves (3) $\frac{3}{4}$" x $9\frac{1}{4}$" x $21\frac{3}{4}$"

Cabinet

$\frac{3}{4}$" Wire brads (24–36)
$1\frac{1}{2}$" x $34\frac{1}{2}$" Piano hinges and mounting screws (2 sets)
$\frac{1}{2}$"-dia. Magnetic catches
Shelving support pins (12–32)
$\frac{1}{2}$" Drawer pulls (4)
$\frac{5}{8}$" Drawer pulls (4)
$\frac{3}{4}$" Drawer pulls (2)
$\frac{3}{8}$" x 1" Dowels (4)

Stand (optional)

#12 x $1\frac{3}{4}$" Roundhead wood screws (4)
$\frac{3}{16}$" Flat washers (4)

*Make this part from plywood.
†Make these parts from pegboard.

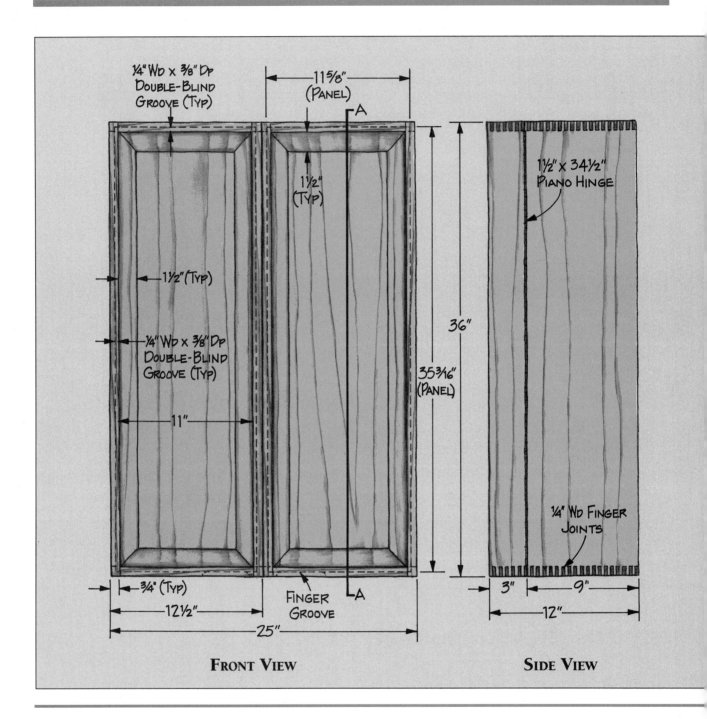

FRONT VIEW   **SIDE VIEW**

PLAN OF PROCEDURE

1 Select the stock and cut the parts to size.
As designed, this cabinet will either hang on a wall or
rest on a stand. Before you purchase the materials,
decide how you want to mount your cabinet. To build
the cabinet *without* the optional stand, you need about
38 board feet of 4/4 (four-quarters) stock, plus partial
sheets of ¼-inch cabinet-grade plywood and ⅛-inch

pegboard. If you build the stand, too, you'll need an
additional 6 board feet of 4/4 stock and 7 board feet
of 8/4 (eight-quarters) stock. You can use any durable
hardwood for the cabinet and stand, such as maple,
beech, or oak. The cabinet shown is made from
figured maple and cherry.

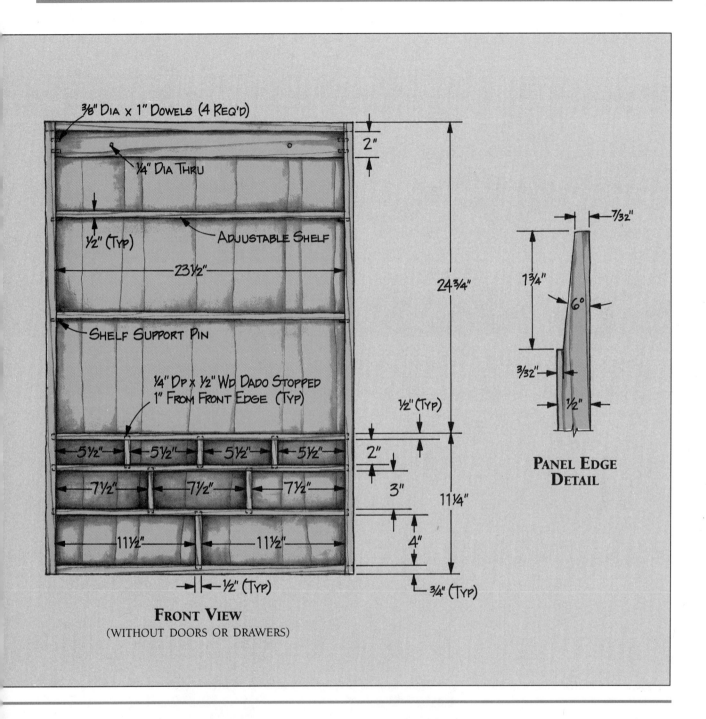

FRONT VIEW
(WITHOUT DOORS OR DRAWERS)

**PANEL EDGE
DETAIL**

Cut the back panel from plywood. Then plane the 4/4 stock to ³/₄ inch thick and cut the case top and bottom, case sides, door tops, door bottoms, door sides, and hanger to the sizes shown in the Materials List. If you're making the stand, also cut out the shelves. Set aside a small amount of ³/₄-inch stock for test pieces, then plane the remainder to ¹/₂ inch thick. Cut the racks, shelves, dividers, and door panels; set aside some extra ¹/₂-inch stock; and plane the remainder to ³/₈ inch thick to make the drawer fronts, backs, and sides. However, *don't* cut the drawer parts yet; wait until after you have assembled the case. If you're making the stand, plane the 8/4 stock to 1¹/₂ inches thick and cut the legs, braces, and feet.

2 Cut the joinery for the case and doors.

The cabinet case and doors are three large boxes. The joinery is fairly simple — the top, bottom, and sides of each box are joined with finger joints; the front panel floats in grooves, and the back rests in rabbets. The inside of the case box is fitted with fixed shelves and dividers, which are joined with blind dadoes. You can make all of these joints with either a router or a dado cutter.

First, cut ¼-inch finger joints in the ends of the case top, bottom, and sides, and in the ends of the door tops, bottoms, and sides. (SEE FIGURES 7-1 THROUGH 7-3.) You must make a jig for either your table saw (if you use a dado cutter) or your router table (if you use a router).

Next, cut ¼-inch-wide, ⅜-inch-deep double-blind grooves in the door parts, on the inside faces near the front edges. Square the ends of the grooves with a chisel. (SEE FIGURE 7-4.) These grooves hold the door panels, as shown in *Section A.* The grooves are blind on each end — that is, they are not cut all the way to the ends of the boards, but stop ⅜ inch from each end. If they were cut all the way through, you'd see them when you assembled the doors.

Cut ¼-inch-wide, ¼-inch-deep double-blind rabbets in the back edges of the case parts in much the same manner as the grooves — stop them ½ inch from each end, and square each blind end with a chisel. These rabbets will hold the back.

Also cut *single*-blind dadoes in the inside faces of the case sides and in the fixed shelves. These dadoes house the fixed shelves in the sides and the dividers in the fixed shelves. Cut the dadoes through to the back edges, but stop them 1 inch before the front edges. Again, square the blind ends with a chisel.

Using a band saw or a table saw, cut 1-inch-long, ¼-inch-deep notches in the front corners of the fixed shelves and dividers. These notches fit around the blind ends of the dadoes.

3 Rout the finger grooves.
Using a router and a ½-inch roundnose bit, rout ½-inch-wide, ⅜-inch-deep double-blind finger grooves in the outside faces of the door bottoms, as shown in the *Finger Groove Detail.* These grooves will serve as pulls to open and close the doors.

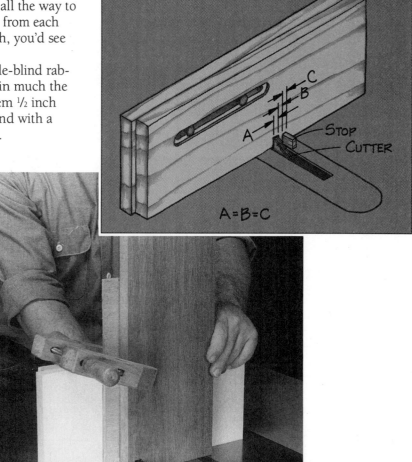

7-1 To cut a finger joint on a table saw or a router table, you must first make an auxiliary miter gauge face with a stop, as shown. The width of the dado cutter (or the diameter of the router bit), the width of the stop, and the distance between the cutter and the stop must all be precisely the same. To make the first cut, place a board against the miter gauge face and butt one edge against the stop. Turn on the saw or router and slide the board forward, cutting the first notch.

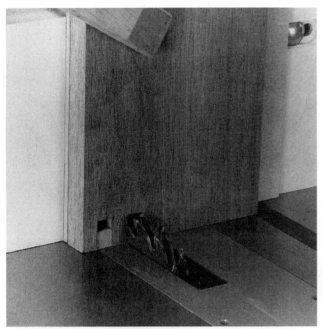

7-2 Move the board sideways until the notch you just cut fits over the stop. (It should fit snug, with no perceptible slop.) Cut a second notch and move the board again. Repeat until you have cut all the notches in the first board.

7-3 To cut the first notch in the adjoining board, use the first board as a spacer. Turn the first board edge for edge and place the first notch over the stop. Butt the second board against the first, turn on the saw or router, and cut the second board, creating a *corner* notch. Remove the first board and continue cutting notches in the second. When you've finished, the notches and the fingers in the two boards should interlock.

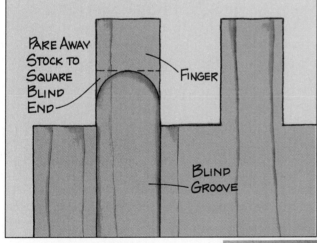

PARE AWAY
STOCK TO
SQUARE
BLIND
END

FINGER

BLIND
GROOVE

7-4 To make a blind groove, stop cutting before you reach the end of the board. To make a *double-blind* groove, don't cut through to *either* end. If you need to square a blind end, cut away the waste with a chisel.

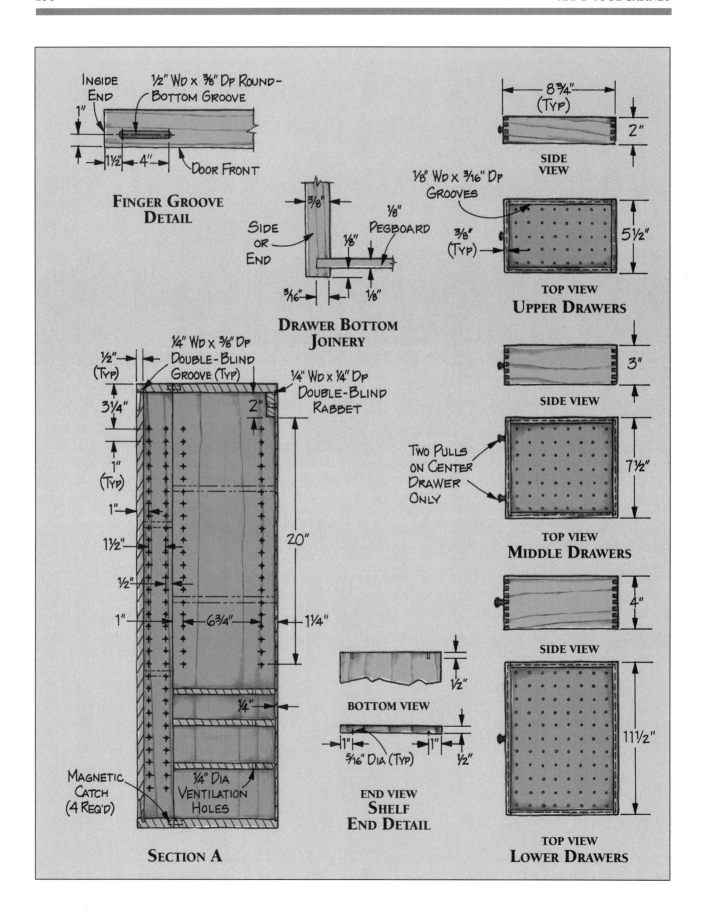

INSIDE END

1"

½" Wₒ x ⅜" Dᴘ ROUND-BOTTOM GROOVE

1½" — 4"

DOOR FRONT

FINGER GROOVE DETAIL

⅜"

SIDE OR END

⅛"

⅛" PEGBOARD

⅛"

³⁄₁₆" ⅛"

DRAWER BOTTOM JOINERY

8¾" (TYP)

2"

SIDE VIEW

⅛" Wₒ x ³⁄₁₆" Dᴘ GROOVES

⅜" (TYP)

5½"

TOP VIEW UPPER DRAWERS

½" (TYP)

¼" Wₒ x ⅜" Dᴘ DOUBLE-BLIND GROOVE (TYP)

¼" Wₒ x ¼" Dᴘ DOUBLE-BLIND RABBET

3¼"

2"

1" (TYP)

1"

1½"

20"

½"

1"

6¾"   1¼"

¼"

MAGNETIC CATCH (4 REQ'D)

¼" DIA VENTILATION HOLES

SECTION A

½"

BOTTOM VIEW

1" 5⁄₁₆" DIA (TYP) 1" ½"

END VIEW SHELF END DETAIL

3"

SIDE VIEW

TWO PULLS ON CENTER DRAWER ONLY

7½"

TOP VIEW MIDDLE DRAWERS

4"

SIDE VIEW

11½"

TOP VIEW LOWER DRAWERS

4 Drill holes for the shelving supports, dowels, and ventilation. The adjustable racks and shelves are held by shelving support pins, which rest in ¼-inch-diameter, ½-inch-deep holes in the case sides and door sides. Lay out the holes as shown in *Section A,* then drill them. Also drill ⅜-inch-diameter, ½-inch-deep dowel holes in the sides and hanger.

Drill ¼-inch-diameter ventilation holes through the fixed shelves about 1 inch from the back edges. The precise location of these holes isn't important, but there should be six to eight of them per shelf. These let the camphor vapors rise from the bottom drawers.

5 Cut the raised panels. The panels in the doors are raised, as shown in the *Panel Edge Detail.* Cut the bevels in the ends and edges of the panel with a table saw. You can also use a table-mounted router or a shaper and a panel-raising cutter.

6 Assemble the case and doors. Dry assemble (*without* glue) the parts of the case and door to check the fit of the joints. When you're satisfied that all the parts fit properly, finish sand them.

Assemble the case first. Join the top, bottom, sides, and hanger with glue, making sure that the parts are perfectly square to one another after you clamp them together. Temporarily tack the back in place with wire brads to hold the case square while the glue dries.

Let the glue set up, then remove the back. Glue the shelves and dividers in the case, sliding first the shelves into their dadoes, and then the dividers.

Assemble the doors one at a time, gluing the door sides, top, and bottom together. Slide the panel into its grooves as you assemble the other parts, but *don't* glue it in place. Let it float in its grooves. As you clamp each door together, also clamp it to the assembled case

where it will later be hinged. (*See Figure 7-5.*) This will ensure that the doors fit the case precisely.

When the glue has dried on the doors, remove them from the case. Attach the back with glue and wire brads. Let the glue dry, then sand all the joints on the case and doors clean and flush.

7 Cut the drawer parts. Measure the openings for the drawers in the assembled case. If they differ from the dimensions shown in the drawings, adjust the sizes of the drawer parts accordingly. Then cut the drawer fronts, backs, and sides from ⅜-inch-thick stock, and the drawer bottoms from ⅛-inch pegboard. **Note:** The holes in the pegboard will let the camphor vapors circulate through the drawers.

FOR BEST RESULTS

Cut the drawer parts so the drawers will be the same size as their openings when assembled. Don't try to build them slightly smaller, even though they need to be ¹⁄₃₂ to ¹⁄₁₆ inch smaller to slide smoothly. Instead, plane or sand the surfaces of the drawers to get a perfect fit.

---

8 Cut the drawer joinery. The drawer parts are joined in exactly the same way as the doors. Cut ¼-inch finger joints in the ends of the fronts, backs, and sides, using a router or dado cutter. Then rout ⅛-inch-wide, ³⁄₁₆-inch-deep double-blind grooves in the inside surfaces of these drawer parts, near the bottom edges. Stop the grooves ⅛ inch from the ends of the boards, but *don't* bother to square the blind ends.

7-5 As you assemble each door, clamp it to the case where it will later be hinged. Make sure the top, the bottom, and the outside side of the door are flush with the case. That way, even if the case is slightly warped or out of square, the doors will still match precisely. **Note:** Put wax paper between the doors and the case to keep them from sticking.

9 **Assemble and fit the drawers.** Assemble the drawers, gluing the fronts, backs, and sides together. Slide the bottoms into their grooves as you assemble the other parts, but *don't* glue them in place. Let them float in their grooves. As you clamp each drawer together, check that it's square.

When the glue is dry, test fit the drawers in their openings. They will probably be too tight, and will bind when they slide in and out. Sand or plane the surfaces until they slide easily.

Attach 1/2-inch pulls to the upper drawers, 5/8-inch pulls to the middle drawers, and 3/4-inch pulls to the lower drawers. Note that the center middle drawer gets *two* pulls, while all the others get just one. This is because the doors wouldn't close if you mounted just one pull in the middle of this drawer.

10 **Hang the doors.** The doors are attached to the case with piano hinges. These are stronger than ordinary butt hinges, and this added strength helps support the weight of any tools you may want to store on the doors. Cut shallow mortises for these hinges in the outside sides of the doors and the case sides. Attach the hinges to the doors, then hang the doors on the case.

Try This Trick

To make sure the hinges are positioned properly, begin by installing just *three* screws per hinge leaf — one at the top, one at the middle, and one at the bottom. Close the doors to see how they fit — all the outside surfaces should be flush. If not, you may have to reposition one or more hinges. Remove the screws, fill the pilot holes with toothpicks and glue, and drill new holes slightly to one side of the old ones. Once the hinges are positioned where you want them, *then* install the remaining screws.

The doors are held closed with small, round magnetic catches. Drill holes for these catches in the inside edges of the door bottoms and tops, near the inside corners. Put dowel centers in these holes, close the doors, and mark the locations of the magnetic plates on the case top and bottom with the centers. Drill round mortises for the plates, then install both the catches and the plates.

11 **Install the adjustable shelves and racks.** The shelves and racks rest on movable pins. To keep

these boards from shifting positions when you open the door or remove tools, their ends have short, blind, round-bottom grooves that fit over the pins, as shown in the *Shelf End Detail*. To make these grooves, clamp two shelves or two racks together, bottom face to bottom face. Drill 5/16-inch-diameter, 1/2-inch-deep holes where the two boards meet — half of each hole in each board. When you take the boards apart, the holes will split and form round-bottom grooves.

Drill holes of various diameters in the racks to hold the tools you want to hang on them. You may want to "relieve" some of the holes — cut slots from the front edge of the rack to the holes — to make it easier to retrieve and replace the tools.

Place shelving support pins in the holes inside the case and the doors wherever you want to hang shelves and racks. Then rest the shelves and racks on the pins. Make sure the pins engage the round-bottom grooves.

12 **Cut the stand joinery and shapes.** The optional stand consists of two trestles joined by three shelves. The legs, feet, and braces are assembled with mortises and tenons, and the shelves rest in dadoes.

To make the mortises, drill 1-inch-diameter, 1-inch-deep holes in the braces and the feet. Then square the corners of each mortise with a chisel. Make the tenons on the ends of the legs by cutting 1-inch-wide, 1/4-inch-deep rabbets in all four sides. The rabbets will form 1-inch-thick, 1-inch-wide, 1-inch-long tenons. Also, cut 3/4-inch-wide, 3/8-inch-deep dadoes in the legs to hold the shelves, and 1 1/8-inch-wide, 1 1/8-inch-long notches in the corners of the shelves to fit the dadoes. Finally, cut the shapes of the legs and braces.

13 **Drill mounting holes in the braces.** The cabinet is attached to the stand with roundhead wood screws and flat washers. Drill 5/16-inch-diameter pilot holes with 3/4-inch-diameter, 3/8-inch-deep counterbores for these screws, as shown in the *Cabinet Stand/ Side View*.

14 **Assemble the stand.** Dry assemble the stand to test the fit of the joints. When you're satisfied they fit properly, finish sand the parts. Glue the legs, feet, and braces together to make the trestles. Let the glue dry, then glue the shelves to the trestle. As you clamp each assembly together, check that it's square.

15 **Finish the cabinet and stand.** Remove the shelves, racks, doors, and drawers from the cabinet, then detach all of the hardware. Do any necessary touch-up sanding, then apply several coats of tung oil

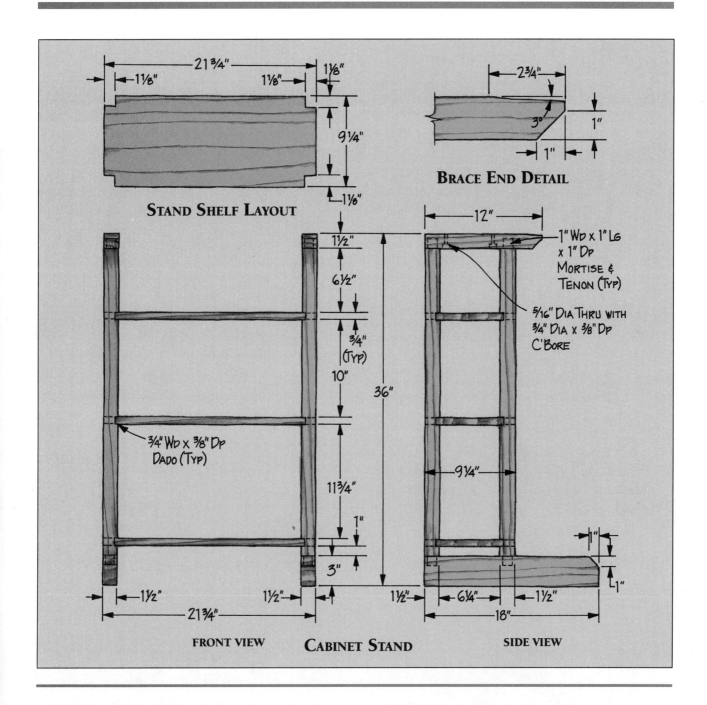

STAND SHELF LAYOUT

BRACE END DETAIL

1" WD x 1" LG x 1" DP MORTISE & TENON (TYP)

5/16" DIA THRU WITH 3/4" DIA x 3/8" DP C'BORE

3/4" WD x 3/8" DP DADO (TYP)

FRONT VIEW   **CABINET STAND**   **SIDE VIEW**

to all wooden surfaces, inside and out, top and bottom. Let the oil dry thoroughly between each coat, and rub out the last coat with #0000 steel wool and paste wax.

If you have elected to build the stand, place the cabinet case on it. Attach the case to the stand by driving #12 x 1¾-inch roundhead wood screws up through the braces and into the case bottom. If you wish to hang the cabinet, first locate the studs in the wall where you plan to mount it. With a helper, hold the cabinet in place on the wall and drill ¼-inch-diameter holes through the hanger over the studs. Then drive ¼-inch lag screws through the hanger and into each stud. Make sure the case is screwed to at least two separate studs.

Replace the hinges and catches on the doors, and hang the doors on the cabinet. Reinstall the pulls on the drawers and replace the drawers in the cabinet. Finally, replace the adjustable shelves and racks in the cabinet, and fill the cabinet with tools.

VARIATIONS

Although the hand tool cabinet will hold almost any small or medium-size tool, this particular cabinet was built to hold planes, scrapers, and chisels. In doing so, the craftsman who made it designed two special shelves to hold the planes. These shelves are angled slightly to make it easier to see and reach the planes. Horizontal stops keep the planes from sliding off, and the shelves are lined with felt to protect the cutting edges of the plane irons. One shelf is made to hold long planes, such as jointer and jack planes, while the other is built for the shorter planes, such as bullnose and rabbet planes.

You may have other tools and accessories that would best be stored on special shelves, racks, or drawers. If so, modify the interior of this cabinet however you see fit.

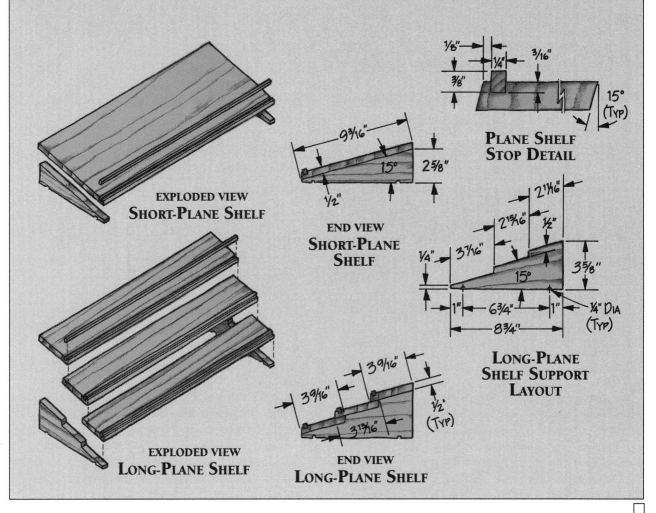

EXPLODED VIEW
SHORT-PLANE SHELF

END VIEW
SHORT-PLANE SHELF

PLANE SHELF STOP DETAIL

LONG-PLANE SHELF SUPPORT LAYOUT

EXPLODED VIEW
LONG-PLANE SHELF

END VIEW
LONG-PLANE SHELF

8

MODULAR WORKBENCH

A good workbench should accommodate you as your woodworking needs change and your skills increase. You should be able to mount additional vises or adapt the storage space for different tools without completely rebuilding the workbench. In other words, your bench should grow with you.

This modular workbench does just that. The design consists of three components — frame, work surface, and cabinet. The trestle frame is sturdy enough to stand up to heavy work, yet there is a great deal of open area between the trestles that can be used for storage. The work surface is large enough to accommodate almost any project, and it will mount a variety of vises and workbench accessories. The cabinet can be fitted with adjustable shelves and various sizes of drawers, and its top is a large, open bin to hold often-used tools. Each component will adapt to your changing needs without having to be rebuilt. And should a component wear out, you can replace it without having to rebuild the entire workbench.

Finally, the workbench is designed to be used anywhere in your shop — against a wall, in a corner, or out in the open. If you use it with one end against a wall or in the open, the drawers and shelves will slide out of the cabinet from both sides, making it easy to reach their contents no matter where you're standing.

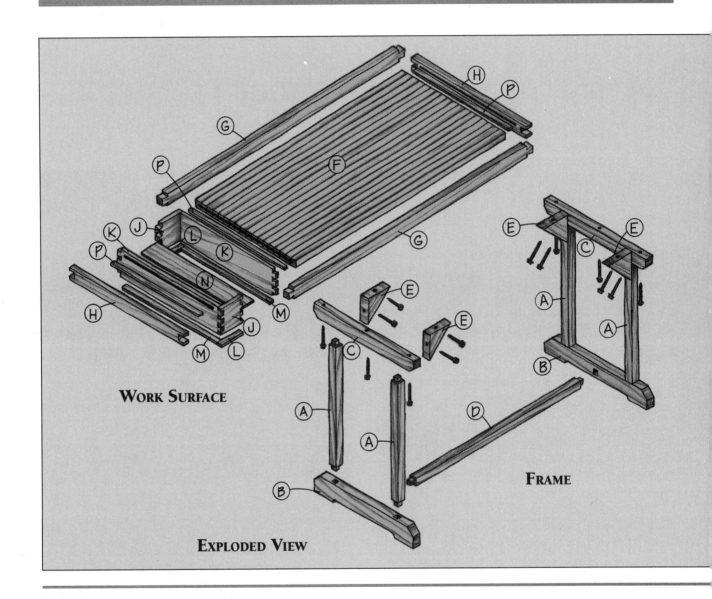

WORK SURFACE

FRAME

EXPLODED VIEW

MATERIALS LIST (FINISHED DIMENSIONS)

Parts

Frame

A. Legs (4)   1¾″ x 1¾″ x 29¼″
B. Feet (2)   1¾″ x 3¾″ x 26½″
C. Battens (2)   1¾″ x 2½″ x 26½″
D. Stretcher   1¾″ x 1¾″ x 44½″
E. Braces (4)   1¾″ x 6″ x 6″

Work Surface

F. Benchtop   1½″ x 27″ x 55¾″
G. Front/back
    trim (2)   1½″ x 2½″ x 64¾″

H. Side
    trim (2)   1½″ x 2½″ x 30″
J. Bin front/
    back (2)   ¾″ x 6″ x 6″
K. Bin sides (2)   ¾″ x 6″ x 27″
L. Front/back bin
    ledges (2)   ½″ x ½″ x 4½″
M. Side bin ledges
    (2)   ½″ x ½″ x 24½″
N. Removable bin
    bottom*   ¼″ x 4⁷/₁₆″ x 25⁷/₁₆″
P. Splines* (3)   ¼″ x ¾″ x 26″

Cabinet

Q. Cabinet
    sides* (2)   ¾″ x 21½″ x 22″
R. Cabinet side edge
    trim (4)   ¾″ x ¾″ x 13¾″
S. Cabinet side
    top trim (2)   ¼″ x ¾″ x 22″
T. Cabinet top/
    bottom* (2) ¾″ x 22″ x 41¾″
U. Cabinet bottom
    trim (2)   ¾″ x ¾″ x 41¾″

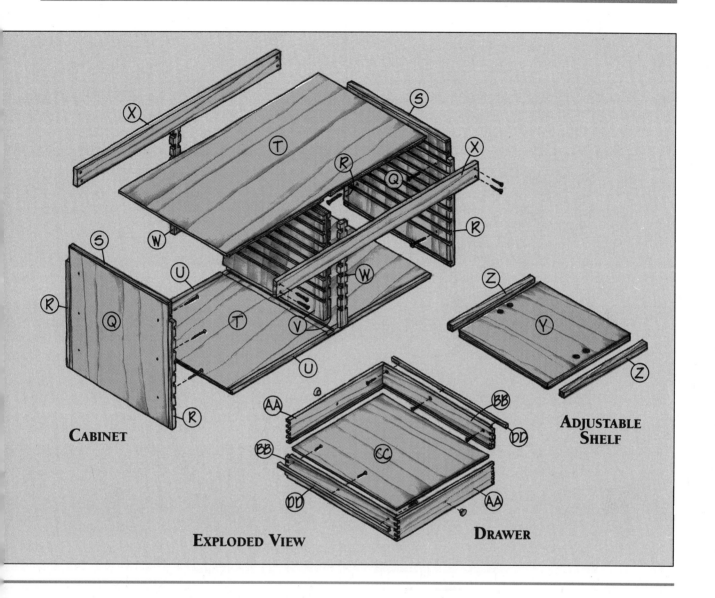

CABINET

ADJUSTABLE SHELF

EXPLODED VIEW

DRAWER

V.	Divider halves* (2)	3/4″ x 22″ x 18³/4″
W.	Divider trim (2)	3/4″ x 1¹/2″ x 18³/8″
X.	Cabinet rails (2)	3/4″ x 3″ x 42¹/2″
Y.	Adjustable shelves* (variable)	1/2″ x 20⁷/16″ x 22″
Z.	Adjustable shelf trim (variable)	1/2″ x 3/4″ x 20⁷/16″
AA.	Drawer fronts/backs (variable)	1/2″ x 2″ x 19³/4″†

BB.	Drawer sides (variable)	1/2″ x 2″ x 23¹/2″†
CC.	Drawer bottoms* (variable)	1/4″ x 19¹/4″ x 23″
DD.	Drawer guides (variable)	3/8″ x 1/2″ x 23¹/2″

*Make these parts from plywood.

†You can make deeper drawers, if desired. However, the depth of the drawers must be a multiple of 2 inches.

Hardware

Frame

3/8″ x 3¹/2″ Lag screws (6)
3/8″ x 4″ Lag screws (8)
3/8″ Flat washers (14)

Cabinet

#6 x 1″ Flathead wood screws (variable)
#8 x 1¹/2″ Flathead wood screws (8)
#12 x 2″ Flathead wood screws (12)
1¹/2″ Pulls (10)

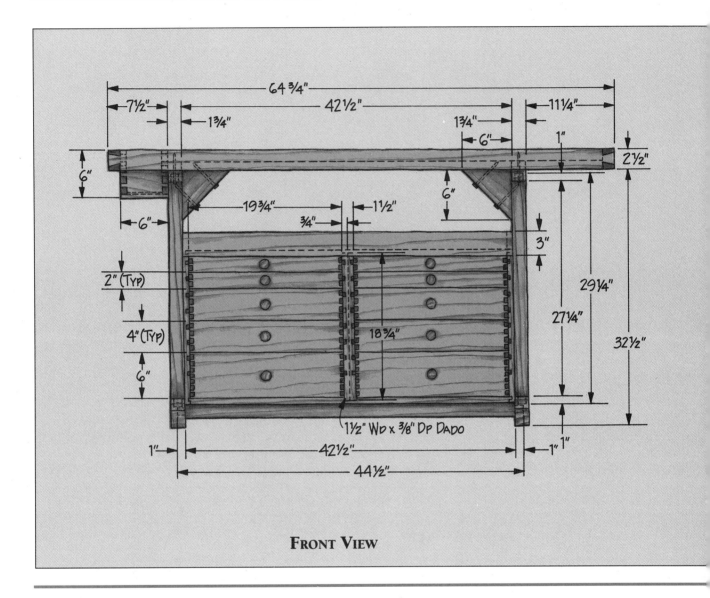

FRONT VIEW

PLAN OF PROCEDURE

1 Select the stock and cut the parts to size. To make the trestle frame for this workbench, you need about 12 board feet of 8/4 (eight-quarters) stock. To make the work surface, you need 32 board feet of 8/4 stock and 4 board feet of 4/4 (four-quarters). To make the cabinet, not including shelves or drawers, you need one 4-foot-by-8-foot sheet of ³/₄-inch plywood and 3 board feet of 4/4 stock. Shelves and drawers will require additional 4/4 stock, ¹/₄-inch plywood, and ¹/₂-inch plywood. The amounts will depend on the number of the shelves and drawers and their sizes.

You can use almost any hardwood and cabinet-grade plywood, although oak, beech, and maple are the traditional choices. On the workbench shown, the frame

is oak, the work surface is hard maple, and the cabinet is birch plywood and maple.

Purchase the lumber needed, then plane the 8/4 stock to 1³/₄ inches thick. Cut the frame parts to size. Set aside some stock for test pieces, and plane the remainder to 1¹/₂ inches thick. Cut the benchtop trim parts and eighteen 1¹/₂-inch-thick, 1¹/₂-inch-wide, 57-inch-long strips. (Later, you'll glue these strips together to make the butcherblock benchtop.) Plane the 4/4 stock to ³/₄ inch thick, and cut the bin front, back, sides, and ledges to size. Cut the bin bottom and splines from ¹/₄-inch plywood. Do *not* cut the cabinet parts until after you have assembled the frame and work surface.

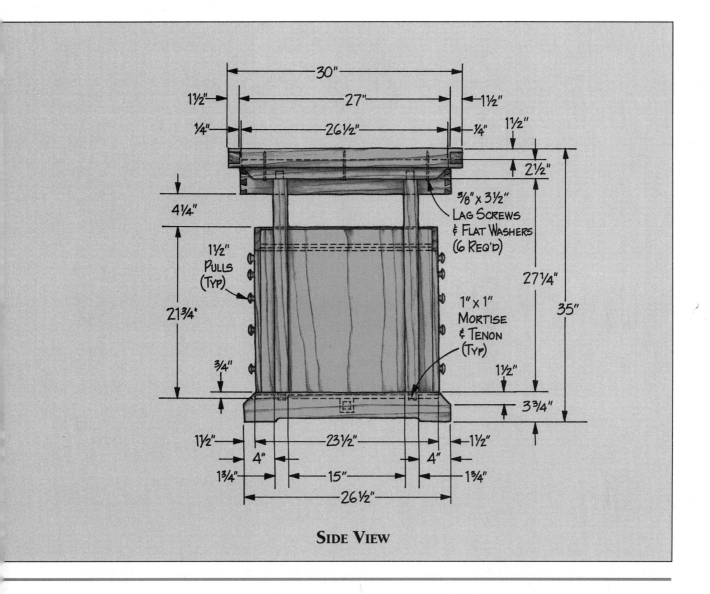

SIDE VIEW

VARIATIONS

If you wish, you can attach casters to the frame of this workbench to make it mobile. However, you may wish to adjust the height of the legs to compensate for the casters.

MAKING THE FRAME

2 Cut the mortises and tenons in the frame parts. Make the frame first so you have some place to rest the work surface and the cabinet. The legs, feet,

battens, and stretcher that make up this assembly are all joined with 1-inch-wide, 1-inch-long, 1-inch-deep mortises and tenons, as shown in the *Side View* and the *Trestle Layout*. To make these joints, first lay out the mortises in the feet and battens. Drill 1-inch-diameter, 1-inch-deep holes to remove most of the waste, and square the mortises with chisels. Using a table-mounted router or a dado cutter, cut tenons in the ends of the legs and stretcher to fit the mortises.

3 Cut the shapes of the feet, battens, and braces. Miter the top corners of the feet and the bottom corners of the battens, as shown in the *Trestle Layout*. Also cut the triangular shapes of the braces. Using a band

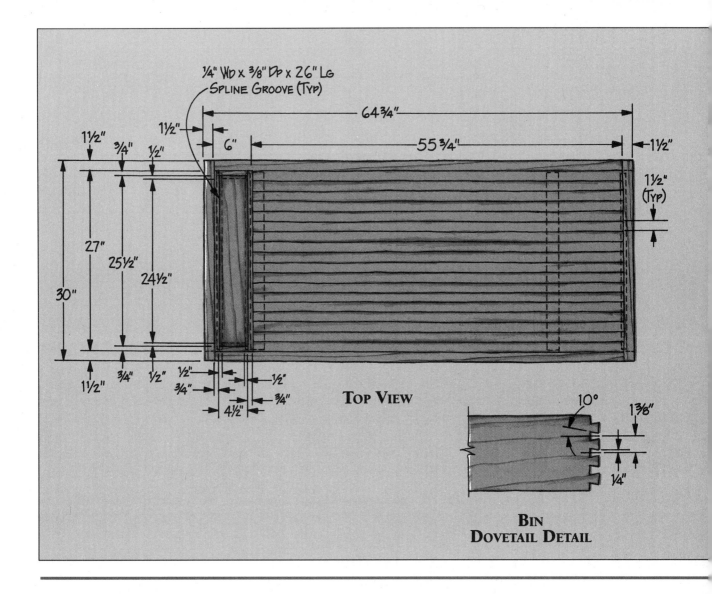

¼" Wᴅ x ⅜" Dᴘ x 26" Lɢ
Sᴘʟɪɴᴇ Gʀᴏᴏᴠᴇ (Tʏᴘ)

Tᴏᴘ Vɪᴇᴡ

Bɪɴ
Dᴏᴠᴇᴛᴀɪʟ Dᴇᴛᴀɪʟ

saw, relieve the bottom of the feet by cutting away ½ inch of stock, creating a pad on each end of each foot. Sand the sawed surfaces to remove the saw marks.

4 Assemble the frame. Dry assemble (*without* glue) the frame to test the fit of the joints. When you're satisfied they fit properly, finish sand the frame parts. Then assemble the legs, feet, and battens with glue to make two trestles. Do *not* attach the braces or glue the stretcher in place until after you've made the cabinet.

MAKING THE WORK SURFACE

5 Assemble the butcherblock benchtop. The benchtop is a butcherblock; that is, all the strips are oriented so the radial grain planes face up. (See "Work-

bench Construction" on page 23 for a complete explanation.) Inspect each strip to determine the radial plane, and mark it. Then glue the strips together. (*SEE FIGURE 8-1.*) Let the glue dry thoroughly, and plane and sand the benchtop smooth. Trim the ends square with a circular saw, cutting the top to length.

6 Cut the dovetails in the bin parts and bench-top trim. The bin front, back, and sides are assembled with through dovetails. Lay out these dovetails, as shown in the *Bin Dovetail Detail*, and cut them by hand or machine (using a table saw, band saw, or router). Also lay out the dovetails on the ends of the benchtop trim parts, as shown in the *Benchtop Trim Dovetail Detail*, and cut them. For these large dovetails, a hand saw or a band saw works best.

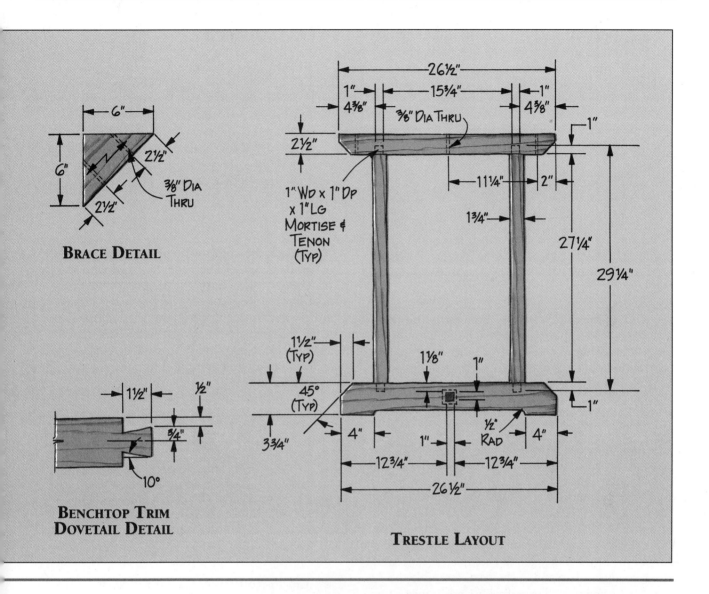

BRACE DETAIL

**BENCHTOP TRIM
DOVETAIL DETAIL**

TRESTLE LAYOUT

8-1 When gluing up the
butcherblock benchtop, the tops and
bottoms of the strips must remain
flush with one another so the finished
benchtop will be flat. To keep the
strips aligned, pinch them together
between several sets of thick, straight
boards, as shown. Separate the benchtop strips and the alignment boards
with wax paper so they won't stick
together.

Note: For the large dovetails on the trim parts, cut the pins on the side trim, and the tails on the front and back trim. *This is extremely important!* If you reverse them, the dovetails will prevent the benchtop from expanding and contracting properly.

VARIATIONS

If you'd rather not cut dovetails, you can substitute finger joints to hold the parts of the bin together, and use bridle joints or mortise-and-tenon joints to join the trim parts. If you use mortises and tenons, cut the tenons in the side trim and the mortises in the front and back trim.

7 **Cut spline grooves in the benchtop and trim.** The bin is held in place by splines. Using a router, cut $\frac{1}{4}$-inch-wide, $\frac{3}{8}$-inch-deep, 26-inch-long spline grooves in both ends of the benchtop, the sides of the bin, and the inside faces of the side trim, as shown in the *Top View*.

8 **Assemble the work surface.** Dry assemble the parts of the work surface to check the fit of the joinery. When you're satisfied that all the pieces fit properly, finish sand all surfaces. Assemble the bin first, gluing the front, back, and sides together. Let the glue set up, and attach the ledges to the inside faces of the bin. The bottom edges of the ledges must be flush with the bottom of the bin. Let the glue dry completely, and sand the glue joints clean and flush. Next, assemble the benchtop, trim parts, bin assembly, and splines with glue. Again, let the glue dry completely and sand all glue joints clean and flush.

FOR BEST RESULTS

Immediately after you've assembled the work surface, and before you build anything else, finish sand it and apply at least two coats of tung oil to all wooden surfaces, top and bottom, inside the bin and out. This will prevent "joint shock" — the damage to joinery that can occur when unfinished assemblies expand or contract rapidly with daily variations in the relative humidity. Wide constructions such as the work surface are particularly vulnerable to joint shock.

MAKING THE CABINET

9 **Cut the cabinet parts.** Assemble the frames, inserting the stretcher in the trestles; then carefully measure the distance between the two trestles. If this distance has changed even a fraction of an inch from what is shown on the drawings, you will have to adjust the size of the cabinet parts to compensate. When you're certain how long to build the cabinet, cut the sides, top, bottom, dividers, rails, and trim to size. *Don't* cut the drawers or shelves yet; wait until the cabinet is assembled.

10 **Attach the trim to the plywood parts.** The plywood parts of the cabinet are trimmed with strips of matching hardwood to hide the plies. Glue the divider halves together face to face to make a single board $1\frac{1}{2}$ inches thick, and let the glue set up. Then glue the trim parts to the divider, sides, and bottom. When the glue dries completely, sand all surfaces flush and clean. Be careful not to sand through the thin plywood face veneer.

TRY THIS TRICK

Make the trim about $\frac{1}{32}$ inch thicker than the plywood, then carefully scrape it flush with the adjoining plywood after gluing it in place. This will help prevent sanding through the plywood veneer.

11 **Cut the joinery in the cabinet parts.** The top, bottom, sides, and divider are all joined with dadoes and rabbets. In addition, the inside faces of the sides and divider are cut with dadoes to hold the shelves and drawers. Make these joints with a router or dado cutter:
- $\frac{3}{8}$-inch-wide, $\frac{3}{8}$-inch-deep dadoes in the sides to hold the cabinet top and bottom, as shown in the *Cabinet Side Layout*
- $\frac{3}{8}$-inch-wide, $\frac{3}{8}$-inch-deep rabbets in the ends of the top and the bottom, creating tenons to fit the dadoes in the sides
- $\frac{1}{2}$-inch-wide, $\frac{3}{8}$-inch-deep dadoes in the sides and divider to hold the shelves and drawers, as shown in the *Divider Layout*
- $1\frac{1}{2}$-inch-wide, $\frac{3}{8}$-inch-deep dadoes in the top and bottom to hold the divider, as shown in the *Front View*

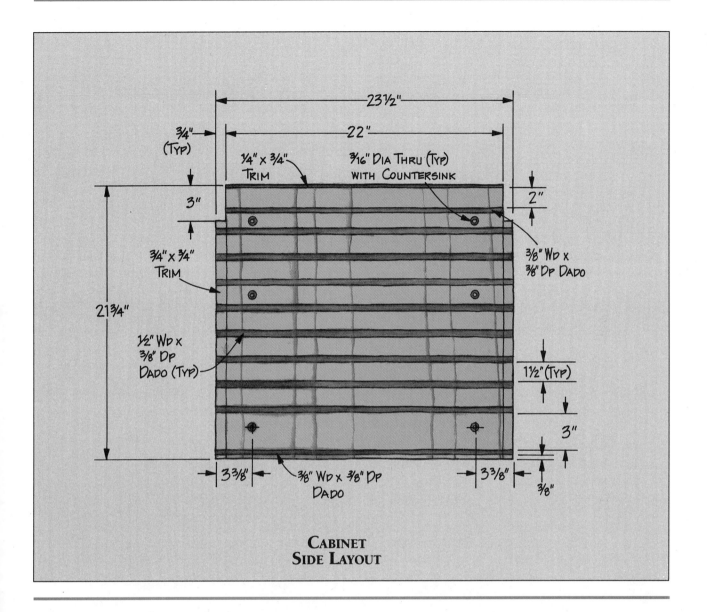

**CABINET
SIDE LAYOUT**

12 Assemble the cabinet case. Dry assemble the parts of the cabinet case, then finish sand them. Assemble the sides, top, bottom, rails, and divider with glue, making sure the assembly is square as you clamp it up. Reinforce the glue joints that hold the rails in place with #8 flathead wood screws. Counterbore and countersink these screws, then cover the heads with wooden plugs. When the glue is dry, cut the plugs flush with the surrounding surfaces. Sand all joints clean and flush.

13 Assemble the frame, cabinet, and work surface. Assemble the trestles and stretcher, then rest the cabinet in the frame to make sure it fits properly. If it does, glue the trestles and stretchers together. Before

the glue dries, attach the cabinet to the frame, driving #12 flathead wood screws from the inside of the case into the legs. Countersink the heads of the screws slightly below the wood surface. Then attach the work surface to the frame, driving 3½-inch-long lag screws up through the battens and into the benchtop. Finally, attach the braces, driving 4-inch-long lag screws through them and into the legs and work surface.

14 Cut the shelf and drawer parts. Decide how many drawers and shelves you'll need and how you want to arrange them. As shown, the cabinet is filled with drawers of different depths — there are no shelves. However, you can build any combination and configuration you wish. The only restriction is that

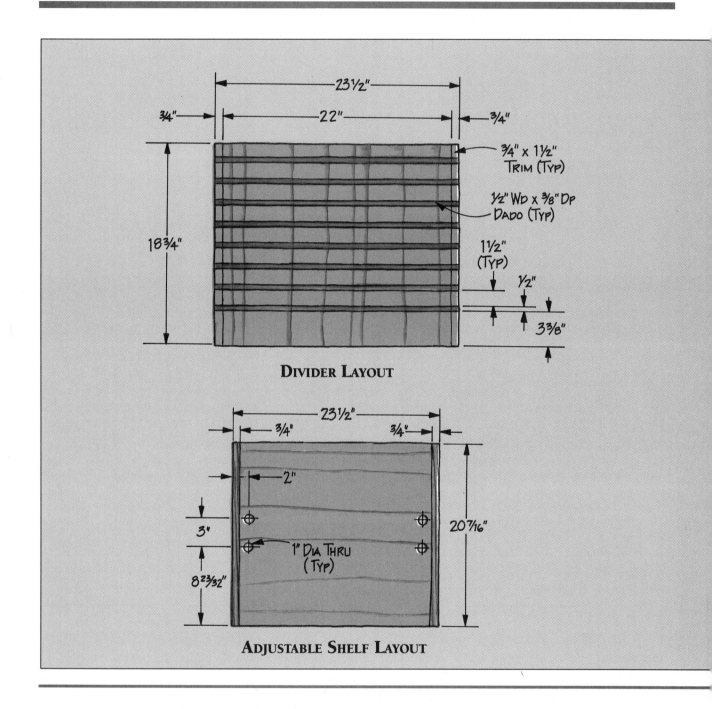

DIVIDER LAYOUT

ADJUSTABLE SHELF LAYOUT

the depths of the drawers *must be divisible by 2 inches.* In other words, the width of the drawer fronts, backs, and sides can only be 2, 4, 6, 8, or some other multiple of 2 inches.

When you know how you will fill the cabinet with drawers and shelves, carefully measure the openings. If the measurements have changed from what is shown on the drawings, adjust the dimensions of the shelf and drawer parts to compensate. Then cut the parts to size.

15 Assemble the shelves. The shelves are pieces of ½-inch plywood that fit in the dadoes and will slide in and out of the cabinet. Glue trim pieces to the ends of these shelves to hide the plies, let the glue dry, and scrape the surfaces flush. Once again, be careful not to cut through the plywood veneer. Drill 1-inch-diameter finger holes, as shown in the *Adjustable Shelf Layout.*

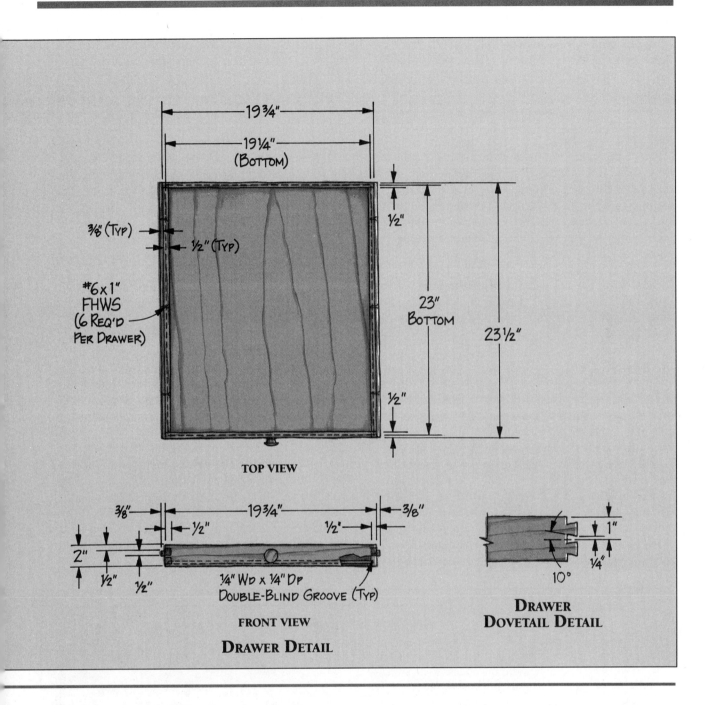

TOP VIEW

¼" Wd x ¼" Dp
Double-Blind Groove (Typ)

FRONT VIEW

DRAWER DETAIL

**DRAWER
DOVETAIL DETAIL**

16 Assemble the drawers. The drawer fronts, backs, and sides are joined with through dovetails. The bottoms rest in grooves in the fronts, backs, and sides. Cut the dovetails by hand or machine, whichever you prefer, as shown in the *Drawer Dovetail Detail.* You may also substitute finger joints for the dovetails, if you wish. Then cut ¼-inch-wide, ¼-inch-deep *double-blind* grooves in the inside faces of the fronts, backs, and sides, as shown in the *Drawer Detail/Front View.* These grooves must stop ¼ inch before each

end of each part — you cannot cut them through to the ends or they will show on the assembled drawers.

Test the fit of the drawer joinery, then finish sand the parts. Assemble the front, back, and sides with glue. Slide the bottoms into their grooves as you do so, but do not glue them in place; let them float in the grooves. Make sure that the drawers are absolutely square and flat as you clamp them up. Let the glue dry, then sand the joints clean and flush.

17 **Fit and hang the drawers.** Test fit the drawers in the cabinet openings. They will probably be a little wide and will bind as you slide them in and out. If this is the case, plane or sand the sides of the drawers until they fit the openings with $^1/_{32}$ to $^1/_{16}$ inch of clearance. Also, attach pulls to both the fronts and backs of the drawers.

Attach the guides to the drawer sides with glue and #6 flathead wood screws. Drive the screws from inside the drawers, through the sides and into the guides. Countersink the heads even with or slightly below the surface. Each guide must be positioned precisely $^1/_2$ inch below the top edge of the drawer, no matter what the depth of the drawer.

Test fit the drawers again, sliding the guides into the dadoes in the sides and the dividers. If any of the drawers bind as you slide them in and out, plane or sand the surfaces that rub until the drawers slide smoothly.

FINISHING UP

18 **Install the vises and other workbench accessories.** When all three modules are completely assembled, install the vises and any other bench hardware you may have. The workbench shown has three vises — one patternmaker's vise and two bench vises. There are also holes for bench dogs, two mounts for a screw holdfast, and several pop-up stops. However, you may not need or want all this paraphernalia. If you're not sure what equipment you do need, start with one vise. Then add vises and other bench accessories as you gain more woodworking experience.

If you have just one vise, mount it on the front of the work surface, near the tool bin. (You may have to remove one of the braces to do this.) Install the second vise on a side, opposite the tool bin and near the front corner. Place the third vise on the same side, near the back corner. Drill or mortise a row of dog holes to use with each vise. Space these holes so they're at least 1 inch closer together than the maximum capacity of the vise. For example, the jaws of the side-mounted bench vises shown open to 7 inches, so the dog holes are spaced every 6 inches.

19 **Finish the workbench.** Remove all the vises and any other workbench accessories that you have installed. Pull out all the shelves and drawers from the cabinet, then disassemble the three components — frame, work surface, and cabinet. Remove all assembly screws and set them aside.

Do any necessary touch-up sanding, then apply several coats of tung oil. For the last coat, mix 2 tablespoons of spar varnish to each cup of tung oil — this will make the final coat of finish very durable. Let the finish cure for several days, then rub it out with #0000 steel wool and paste wax. The wax helps the bench resist spilled glue and chemicals.

20 **Reassemble the workbench.** After finishing the components, reassemble the frame, cabinet, and work surface. Place the bottom in the bin and slide the shelves and drawers back into the cabinet. Finally, reinstall the vises and other equipment. If you wish, mount casters to the outside surfaces of the frame to make the workbench mobile.

TRY THIS TRICK

If you must make square dog holes, it's easier to do so *before* you assemble the benchtop than afterwards. Cut or rout notches in the edges of the appropriate strips before gluing up the butcherblock. These notches will become square dog holes after the strips are laminated.

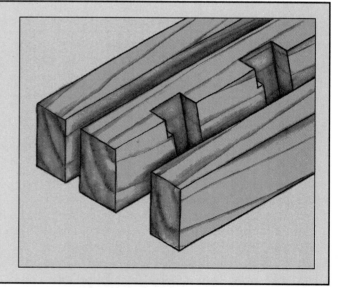

9

ADJUSTABLE SHOP STOOL

While workbenches and tool cabinets help make a shop a pleasant place to work, nothing provides so much comfort as a chair or a stool. Although most woodworking tasks are accomplished standing up, there are many jobs that you might do better and work at longer sitting down. And there are other times when it feeds your woodworking soul just to sit and admire your own craftsmanship. This adjustable shop stool provides a place to do that.

The seat of the stool adjusts from 16 inches (chair height) to 27 inches high (stool height). A tool bin beneath the seat can be adjusted

independently of the seat height. To change the position of the seat or the bin, remove the carriage bolts that hold it in place, move it to the desired height, and replace the bolts.

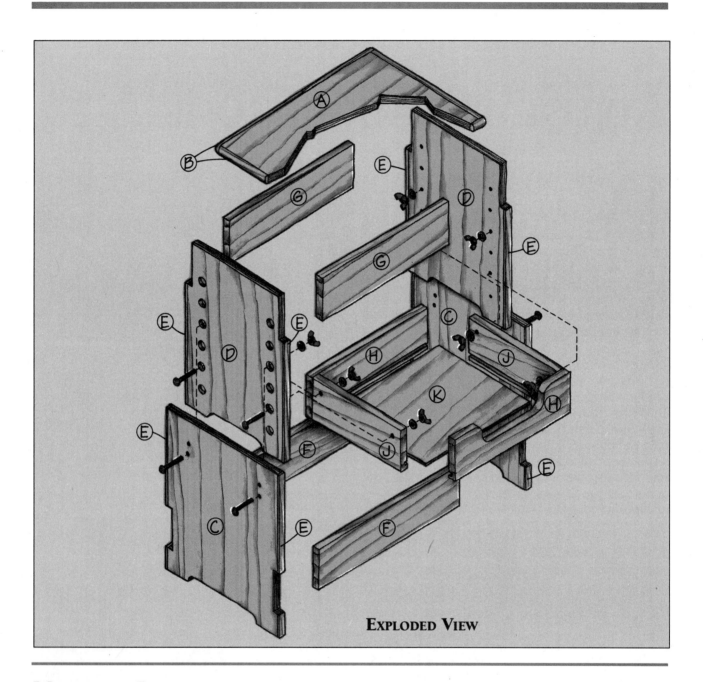

EXPLODED VIEW

MATERIALS LIST (FINISHED DIMENSIONS)

Parts

A. Seat*   ³/₄″ x 13″ x 17″
B. Seat trim
   (total)   ¹/₂″ x ³/₄″ x 70″
C. Standing supports*
   (2)   ³/₄″ x 12¹/₂″ x 15¹/₄″
D. Adjustable supports*
   (2)   ³/₄″ x 11″ x 15¹/₄″
E. Support trim
   (total)   ¹/₄″ x ³/₄″ x 128″

F. Standing support
   rails (2)   ³/₄″ x 4″ x 16″
G. Adjustable support
   rails (2)   ³/₄″ x 4″ x 14¹/₂″
H. Bin sides (2)   ³/₄″ x 4″ x 13″
J. Bin ends (2)   ³/₄″ x 4″ x 10″
K. Bin bottom*   ¹/₄″ x 10¹/₂″ x 12″

Make these parts from plywood.

Hardware

#8 x 1¹/₄″ Flathead wood screws
   (32)
³/₈″ x 2″ Carriage bolts (8)
³/₈″ Flat washers (8)
³/₈″ Wing nuts (8)

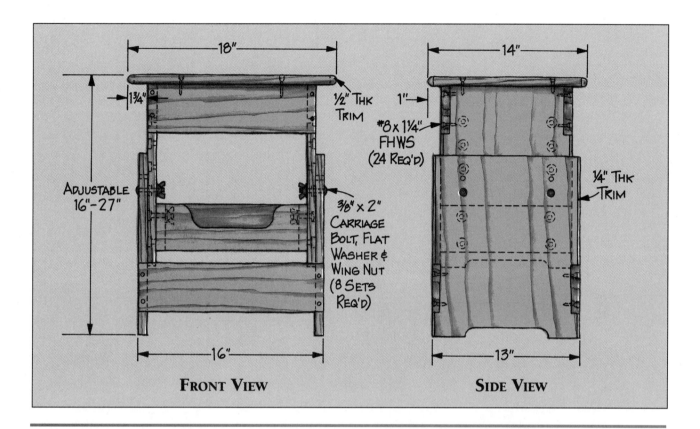

FRONT VIEW   **SIDE VIEW**

PLAN OF PROCEDURE

1 Select the stock and cut the parts to size.

To make this stool, you need about 4 board feet of 4/4 (four-quarters) stock, one half-sheet (4 feet by 4 feet) of ³/₄-inch plywood, and a scrap of ¹/₄-inch plywood. You can use any durable hardwood and cabinet-grade plywood. The stool shown is built from maple and birch-veneer plywood.

Plane the 4/4 stock to ³/₄ inch thick, then cut the parts to size. Also, rip the trim from the ³/₄-inch-thick stock. Glue the ¹/₂-inch-thick trim to the ends and edges of the seat, and the ¹/₄-inch-thick trim to the edges of the supports. Let the glue dry, then scrape the trim flush with the plywood. Be careful not to scrape through the plywood veneer.

TRY THIS TRICK

Hold the trim in place with masking tape while the glue dries. Masking tape is slightly elastic, and by spacing the tape pieces every 1 to 2 inches, you can generate adequate clamping pressure to form a strong glue bond.

2 Drill the bolt holes in the supports and bin ends.

Stack the standing supports face to face with the ends and edges flush, and secure them temporarily with double-faced carpet tape. Do the same for the adjustable supports and the bin ends. Lay out the bolt holes on these pieces, as shown in the *Standing Support Layout, Adjustable Support Layout,* and *Bin/Side View.*

Drill ³/₈-inch-diameter bolt holes through the standing supports and the bin ends. Drill ¹/₈-inch-diameter holes through the adjustable supports where you've marked the bolt holes. This will transfer the hole locations to the other side of the stack. Drill ⁷/₈-inch-diameter, ³/₈-inch-deep counterbores in one adjustable support, turn the stack over, and drill them in the other. Then drill ³/₈-inch-diameter bolt holes through the centers of the counterbores. Do not take the stacks apart yet.

3 Cut the shapes of the supports and bin side.

Lay out the notches and the shapes of the feet on the supports, as shown in the *Standing Support Layout* and *Adjustable Support Layout.* Also, lay out the shape of the front bin side, as shown in the *Bin/Front View.* Cut

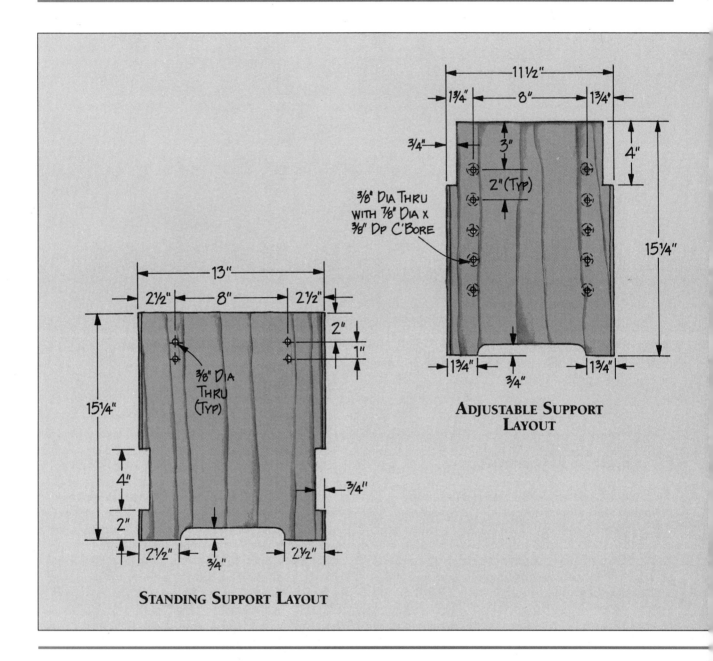

ADJUSTABLE SUPPORT LAYOUT

STANDING SUPPORT LAYOUT

these shapes with a saber saw or band saw. Sand the sawed edges to remove the saw marks, then take the stacked pieces apart and discard the tape.

4 Cut the grooves in the bin parts. The bin bottom rests in ¼-inch-wide, ¼-inch-deep grooves in the bin sides and ends, as shown in the *Bin/Side View.* Cut these grooves with a router or a dado cutter.

5 Round over the edges of the seat. The edges of the seat are rounded to make it more comfortable. Do this rounding with a router and a ³⁄₈-inch-radius

roundover bit. **Note:** Make sure the glue that holds the trim to the seat has dried for *at least* 24 hours before routing.

6 Assemble the stool. Finish sand all the parts. Then assemble the bin sides and ends with glue and screws. Countersink and counterbore the screws so the heads rest about ⅛ inch below the wood surface. As you put these parts together, slide the bottom into its grooves, but do *not* glue the bottom in place. Let the glue dry, then sand the joints clean and flush.

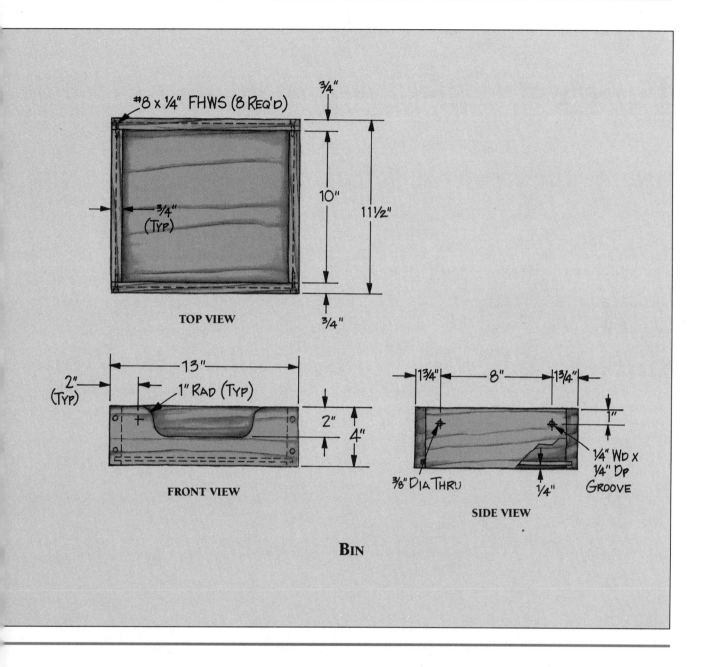

#8 x 1/4" FHWS (8 Req'd)

3/4"

10"

11½"

3/4" (TYP)

3/4"

TOP VIEW

2" (TYP)

13"

1" RAD (TYP)

2"

4"

FRONT VIEW

1¾"   8"   1¾"

1"

⅜" DIA THRU   ¼"

¼" WD X ¼" DP GROOVE

SIDE VIEW

BIN

Bolt the bin to the adjustable sides with carriage bolts, washers, and wing nuts. It doesn't matter where you attach these parts, but use the same set of holes in each adjustable support so the supports are at the same level. Then bolt the standing supports to the adjustable supports. Again, it doesn't matter where, but use the same sets of holes for each pair of supports. Attach the rails to the standing supports with glue and screws, then do the same for the adjustable supports. Rest the assembly on its feet and attach the seat with glue and screws. Remember to countersink and counterbore each screw.

Cover all the heads of the screws with wooden plugs. Let the glue dry, then sand the joints and the plugs clean and flush.

7 Finish the stool. Remove all the carriage bolts, breaking down the stool into three subassemblies — stand, seat, and bin. Do any necessary touch-up sanding, then apply several coats of tung oil to all wooden surfaces. Let the last coat cure completely, and rub it out with fine steel wool and paste wax. Reassemble the stool, adjusting the seat and the bin to whatever height you find comfortable.

INDEX

Note: Page references in *italic* indicate photographs or illustrations.

WOODWORKING GLOSSARY

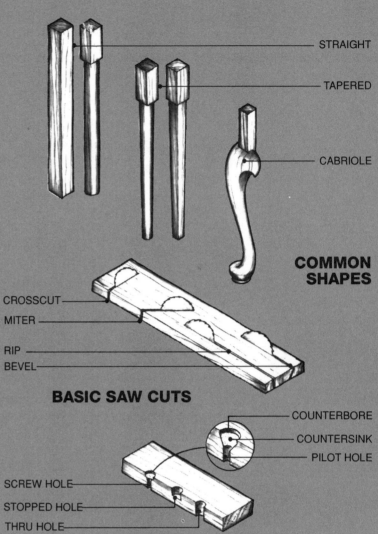

COMMON SHAPES

STRAIGHT

TAPERED

CABRIOLE

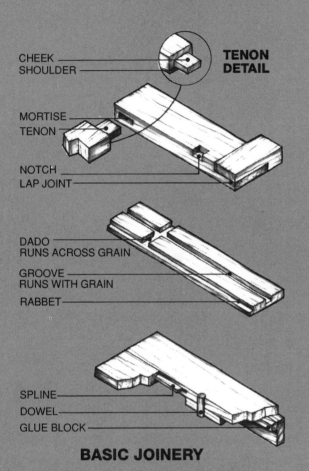

TENON DETAIL

CHEEK
SHOULDER

MORTISE
TENON

NOTCH
LAP JOINT

DADO
RUNS ACROSS GRAIN

GROOVE
RUNS WITH GRAIN

RABBET

SPLINE
DOWEL
GLUE BLOCK

BASIC JOINERY

CROSSCUT
MITER

RIP
BEVEL

BASIC SAW CUTS

COUNTERBORE
COUNTERSINK
PILOT HOLE

SCREW HOLE
STOPPED HOLE
THRU HOLE

HOLES

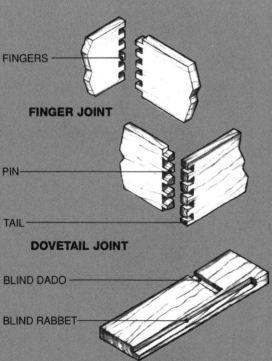

FINGERS

FINGER JOINT

PIN

TAIL

DOVETAIL JOINT

BLIND DADO

BLIND RABBET

SPECIAL JOINERY

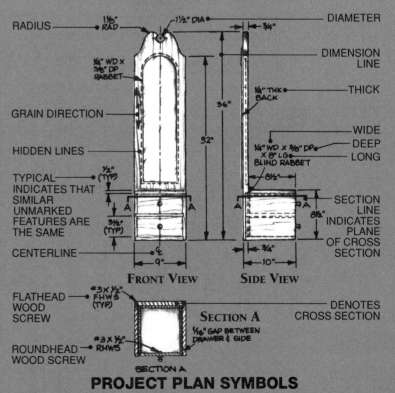

RADIUS — 1⅛" RAD — 1½" DIA — ¾" — DIAMETER

¼" WD × ⅜" DP RABBET

36"

¼" THK BACK — THICK

DIMENSION LINE

GRAIN DIRECTION

32"

WIDE
¼" WD × ⅜" DP × 8" LG BLIND RABBET — DEEP — LONG

HIDDEN LINES

8½"

TYPICAL INDICATES THAT SIMILAR UNMARKED FEATURES ARE THE SAME

½" (TYP)

A

A

SECTION LINE INDICATES PLANE OF CROSS SECTION

3½" (TYP)

8½"

CENTERLINE

¢

9"

¾"
10"

FRONT VIEW

SIDE VIEW

FLATHEAD WOOD SCREW

#3 × ½" FHWS (TYP)

SECTION A
1/16" GAP BETWEEN DRAWER & SIDE

DENOTES CROSS SECTION

ROUNDHEAD WOOD SCREW

#3 × ½" RHWS

SECTION A

PROJECT PLAN SYMBOLS